COMMUNICATING
in the Classroom

Contributing Editor

Clive Sutton   School of Education, University of Leicester

Contributors

Peter Benton   Department of Educational Studies, University of Oxford
Chris Dawson   Department of Education, University of Adelaide
Mike English   Department of English, Leicester Polytechnic
Norma George   Language Centre, Leicestershire Education Authority
Allan Jones   Blackburn Teachers' Centre
Trevor Kerry   Charlotte Mason College, Ambleside
Roger Knight   School of Education, University of Leicester
Owen Watkins   School of Education, University of Leicester

HODDER AND STOUGHTON
LONDON SYDNEY AUCKLAND TORONTO

COMMUNICATING
in the Classroom

A guide for subject teachers on the more effective
use of reading, writing and talk

Contributing Editor: Clive Sutton

British Library Cataloguing in Publication Data

Communicating in the classroom
   1. Teacher-student relationships
   2. High-school teachers – Great Britain
   3. High-school students – Great Britain
   I. Sutton, Clive
   371.11′02   LB1033

ISBN 0 340 26659 7

Printed and bound in Great Britain for
Hodder and Stoughton Educational,
a division of Hodder and Stoughton Ltd,
Mill Road, Dunton Green, Sevenoaks, Kent,
by Robert Hartnoll Ltd, Bodmin.

Contents

Preface

This book is one of the outcomes of a four-year research and development project funded by the Department of Education and Science at the Universities of Leicester, Nottingham and Exeter. The Teacher Education Project set out to examine certain parts of the training of graduates for teaching in secondary schools, and to develop related teaching materials. We deliberately chose topics which for one reason or another now command particular attention in professional preparation — topics such as language for learning, or the teacher's management of mixed ability classes — and this volume collects together the materials on language. Workbooks on the other topics (listed at the end of this preface) are also available.

We should like to acknowledge the very great debt we owe to the host universities, to the Department of Education and Science, and to colleagues and students who have used and criticised earlier drafts. Many individuals have influenced the form of the chapters which appear in this book, and to some we should like to express particular thanks.

We have been ably supported by Trevor Kerry as full-time Research Fellow throughout the period of the project's work. We have also had the support and advice of a Consultative Committee which included Mr A.J. Davis (Leicestershire Education Authority), Prof. Jim Eggleston (Nottingham University), Miss Valerie Evans HMI, Prof. Paul Hirst (Cambridge University), Mr Derek Holford (Leicester University), Mr M. Hutchinson (Frank Wheldon School), Mr R. Seckington (Earl Shilton Community College), Dr D. Sharples (Worcester College), Mr D. Wilkins (Nottinghamshire Education Authority), Prof. D. Wright (Leicester University) and Mr A.G.B. Woollard (D.E.S.). Mrs Audrey Dunning not only typed all the trial materials on language and supervised their distribution and trial, but has also ably prepared the manuscript of *Communicating in the Classroom*.

We should also like to thank the many teachers and student teachers who have sent examples of pupils' written work. To preserve the anonymity of individual pupils only the writers' first names, or in some cases a changed name, have been given.

Other materials prepared in the Teacher Education Project are available as workbooks from Macmillan Publishing Co., dealing with the topics of *Class Management and Control; Teaching Mixed Ability Classes; Handling Group Work; Teaching Bright Pupils and Slow Learners; Effective Questioning and Explaining*.

C.R. Sutton and E.C. Wragg
Joint Directors, Teacher Education Project

Acknowledgements

The authors and publisher wish to thank the following for permission to reproduce material in this book:

R.V.Bateman for his letter in Panel 1. 16; Batsford Academic and Educational Ltd for Panels 2.1 and 2.11 from *Ideas for Teaching History* by Sean Healy, 1974; Blackie and Son Ltd for Panel 2.4 from *Journey into Maths, Book 1* by Alan Bell *et al.,* 1978, and the South Nottinghamshire Project by Alan Bell, Alan Wigley and David Rooke for Panels 1.12 and 2.4; Cambridge University Press for part of Panel 5.7 from *The Major Achievements of Science* by A.E.E. McKenzie, 1960, and for Panel 9.5 from *School Mathematics Project, Book B,* 1970; R.W. Campbell for the letter in Panel 6.2; Charles E. Merrill Publishing Co. for the material in Chapter 4 from *Freedom to Learn* by Carl R. Rogers, 1969; Dover Publications Inc. for the cartoon in Chapter 9, 'Portrait of a Small Boy Reading' from *The Best of Gluyas Williams,* 1971; the Publications Branch of the Education Department of South Australia for the material in Chapter 9 from *Learning in Science,* 1975; Faber and Faber for Panel 1.1 Script A from *Good Enough for the Children* by John Blackie; Mr Phil Findlay, Hinchingbrooke School for the Physics scripts in Chapter 2; Granada Publishing Ltd for Panel 9.4 from *History Alive 1* by Peter Moss, 1969; Heinemann Educational Books for Panels 9.1 and 9.2 from *Physics is Fun, Books 1 and 3* by Jim Jardine, 1964 and 1966; Hutchinson Publishing Group Ltd for Panel 9.6 from *The Geography of Towns* by Arthur E. Smailes, 1953; London Express News and Feature Services for the cartoon by Baxter in Chapter 2; Methuen and Co. Ltd for the extract in Chapter 7 from *O level Cookery* by P.M. Abbey and G.M. McDonald, 1976; John Murray (Publishers) Ltd for Panels 5.7 and 9.3 from *Introduction to Biology* by D.G. MacKean, 1962; the National Association for the Teaching of English for Panel 1.1 Script B from *English in Education, 5, 2;* Oxford University Press for the text in Panel 9.2 from Oxford Social Geographies Book 1 *Poverty and Wealth in Cities and Villages* by Martin Simons, 1975; Mr Stewart Robertson for his letter in Panel 1.16; L.C. Snell for the letter in Panel 6.2; the University of London Institute of Education for material in Panels 1.4, 1.5, 1.8, 2.6 and 2.7 from study units in language in the Schools Council/London University Writing Across the Curriculum Project; Ward Lock Educational for Panels 1.5 and 2.8 from *Writing and Learning Across the Curriculum* by Nancy Martin *et al.,* 1976, and for Panel 1.15 from *Language Across the Curriculum* by Mike Torbe, 1976; Nancy Wilkinson for her letter in Panel 6.2; Panels 9.7 and 9.8 are adaptations of "How Easy? How Interesting?", charts from *The Art of Readable Writing,* Revised Edition by Rudolf Flesch. Copyright 1949, © 1974 by Rudolf Flesch, reprinted by permission of Harper and Row, Publishers Inc.; Panel 5.5 is from *The Epistle of Paul to the Romans* by C.H. Dodd, reprinted by permission of Hodder and Stoughton,© 1932 C.H. Dodd; Panel 1.13 is reproduced by permission from James Britton *et al., The Development of Writing Abilities 11-18,* (Schools Council Research Studies) Macmillan Education, 1975; Panel 1.15 is from *The Paint House* (Penguin Education, 1972) p.43, by Peter McGuire and Susie Daniels © The Paint House, 1972; Panels 1.4, 2.2 and 2.5 are from *Understanding Children Writing* (Penguin Education, 1973) pp.98, 159 and 54, by Carol Burgess, *et al.* Copyright © Carol Burgess, Tony Burgess, Liz Cartland, Robin Chambers, John Hedgeland, Nick Levine, John Mole, Bernard Newsome, Harold Smith, Mike Torbe, 1973; Panel 3.5 is from *From Communication to Curriculum* (Penguin Education, 1976) pp.54-6, by Douglas Barnes. Copyright © Douglas Barnes 1975. These above reprinted by permission of Penguin Books Ltd.

Introduction:
Making Sense of New Ideas

Clive Sutton

Let me try to state in a few sentences one of the main ideas behind this book. It is that people have to *make sense* of any new experience before their knowledge of it is of any use to them. So if you are teaching for understanding, somehow you have to encourage and provoke the sorts of talking, writing, reading and listening that will help the sense-making process. How can it be done? ... and how can we avoid the kinds of language use in the classroom which disallow or discourage it?

Our main focus of attention is on the pupils' language rather than that of the teacher. We are interested in how to maintain the learner's confidence in using language as 'a tool for thinking with'. Of course, the ability to communicate well is important in its own right, and people hope that school leavers will be articulate, and able to explain their thoughts. But it seems that these skills are *also* the key to success in mastering those thoughts in the first place. The struggle to communicate what you want to say is one of the most powerful provocations to sorting out what you understand. So the teacher of physics or geography, mathematics, biology or whatever, has an interest in developing those skills just as much as does the teacher of 'English'. To put it another way: it is *language-for-learning* as well as *language-for-telling-others* that concerns us.

The need for this book and others like it arises because when a knowledgeable teacher meets less knowledgeable pupils it *looks* as if the main function of language is to pass over to the pupils something that the teacher already 'has'. But can knowledge be just passed over in that way? We think not. The teacher's statement is important. But the job is not finished when the pupils listen to it or write it down. The authors of a report on British schooling in 1975 wrote this:

> It is a confusion of everyday thought that we tend to regard 'knowledge' as something that exists independently of someone who knows. 'What is known' must in fact be brought to life afresh within every 'knower' by his own efforts.*

*For detailed references to the Bullock Report *A Language for Life,* and to other sources which have provided inspiration for this work, see the bibliographies at the end of individual chapters.

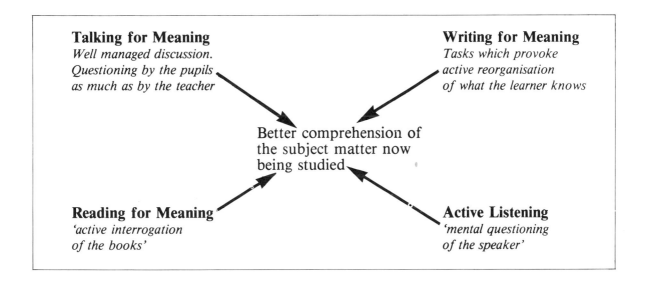

Talking for Meaning
Well managed discussion.
Questioning by the pupils
as much as by the teacher

Writing for Meaning
Tasks which provoke
active reorganisation
of what the learner knows

Better comprehension of the subject matter now being studied

Reading for Meaning
'active interrogation
of the books'

Active Listening
'mental questioning
of the speaker'

It is a powerful statement, summing up the experience of many teachers who have observed children talking themselves into understanding. On the more theoretical side it is supported by developments in cognitive psychology and in the study of language and thought over the last twenty-five years, which have resulted not so much in a different theory of learning as in a redefinition of knowledge. There is a heightened awareness of knowledge as a human creation, and this is linked with the realisation that each learner has to construct or reconstruct it for himself. If knowledge in one sense is food, the learner has first to take it apart (digest it) and then to build it into his existing structures of understanding. It only becomes meaningful once it is integrated with what he already knows.

Such a view is at the heart of all the tactics suggested in this book. Meaning is gained when the learner reflects on experience, and re-orders his own thoughts. That will include reflecting on what he or she knows from outside the school and relating it with what the school offers, thinking over the practical work done in a science lesson, and the books one has read, as well as what the teacher said.

Sometimes all this happens without the teacher having to worry about it. It happens at home, or in the playground, or quietly in the minds of pupils who might seem to be just passively listening. The stimulus of practical work, or the way the teacher kindles the imagination with his or her own presentation of ideas, can start the process. Then, for some, their own desire to understand will keep it going. But many people have come to the conclusion that it doesn't happen enough. Secondary schools are subject to criticism for providing too little opportunity for the pupils to reformulate what they know, and for making too little demand on them to do so, either inside or outside lesson time. Indeed in some subjects existing methods of working may positively discourage restatement, by offering ready-made summaries and allowing pupils to think that the job has then been done.

In defence, most of us could find counter-examples where pupils certainly *do* think things through, talk things out, and write to clarify their own understanding. When it doesn't happen one can claim extenuating circumstances, such as the limited time in lessons, each with its weight of information to be 'got over', or the crowded syllabus to be 'got through'. There is also the seeming inability of some of the pupils to re-express ideas for themselves, especially in writing. Or is it inexperience? Anyway, they fail. That forces one into giving more and more to them, and demanding less and less of them. But even in the choice of words 'got over' and 'got through', we see the dominant influence of an unbalanced theory about the functions of language — the idea that it is just a vehicle for passing on a message.

One of the consequences of this kind of criticism has been a growing interest in small group discussion. *Each* pupil has a chance to say 'It's like such-and-such', or 'Is it like so-and-so?', or 'The difference is ...' and by comparisons and contrasts to begin to relate the new knowledge with the old. But of course it is not quite as easy as that. Some events turn into non-discussions or futile discussions. Chapters 3 and 4 are about how to get better value from such activity.

Another result is a renewed emphasis on writing that is the pupil's own composition, not just in 'English' lessons, but in all subjects. How can a wider range of pupils come to enjoy it, and succeed at it? You will see from Chapters 1 and 2 that it's not just a matter of setting an appropriate task. How one marks the resulting script may be even more important, if children's belief in their own thinking ability is to grow. Trying to foster that belief as well as their fluency and accuracy in the subject could produce conflicts, whose mismanagement may result in neither objective being achieved. For that reason we have placed the discussion of how to respond first, before the discussion of ways of setting interesting and varied work.

As Peter Benton says in Chapter 1, policies on marking *matter*. The form in which the teacher gives marks or makes comments on the pupil's scripts can have cumulative effects beyond those probably intended, and it is important to think just what one is rewarding by the way one marks. Certainly the pupils tune in very quickly to what is acceptable and shape their writing accordingly, and not necessarily in a way which best helps their learning.

In Chapter 2 Owen Watkins reminds us how difficult writing can be, and of the need to help pupils with it if they are to gain the confidence to use it well. Part of that help can come from a clearer discussion beforehand of what the writing is for, and by changing the audience sometimes, to heighten the writer's awareness of what he is trying to say. This chapter also raises the question of

Language and Useful Knowledge. Some ideas to test against your own experience.

---

1   Knowledge reformulated by the learner for himself is

(a)   more easily recalled,

(b)   linked to other knowledge, and so accessible from other points in his thought patterns,

(c)   more easily *used* in daily living, or when solving a problem, in some other field of thought,

(d)   influential upon future perceptions, and an aid to further learning in the subject.

2   Knowledge that the learner does not reformulate is

(a)   more easily forgotten,

(b)   usually remembered only in situations very like those where it was learned,

(c)   not applied or used elsewhere.

3   Reformulation may be provoked

(a)   by small group discussion (in appropriate circumstances),

(b)   by any writing which is the pupil's own composition, as long as pupils and teachers *expect* such reformulation, and the relationships between them allow it and encourage it.

---

whether one may get a better quality of thinking by encouraging the relatively unshaped diaristic writing in which the writer's feelings and reactions to his topic are mixed in with the informative aspect of what he says. Wherever children's writings are shown in either of these chapters, they appear with the original corrections and mistakes, even if they have been put into typescript for economy of space.

In Chapter 3 Mike English surveys the argument for more pupil talk, and provides practical ideas to help the reader appraise its feasibility, while in Chapter 4 Trevor Kerry offers the reader a means of appraising his or her own skill in managing different kinds of discussion. We have deliberately chosen to deal mainly with the rationale for pupil talk. That does not mean that we decry expository teaching; only that effective learning requires a blend of statement by teacher and by pupil. A great deal has been written about teachers' language and the processes of classroom interaction (for example about the influence of questioning style on the pupils' willingness to contribute), and about non-verbal signals in the classroom. Those studies are referred to relatively briefly in this book, in order to focus on the other aspect.

Chapter 5 rounds off the first part of the book with the idea that secondary school teachers can still give pupils a great deal of help over reading and listening, so that they develop the habit of reading, and listening, for understanding.

The later chapters contain a number of shorter activities which have been used on initial and in-service teacher-training courses for starting discussion of the relevant aspects of language. There is material on the assessment of textbooks, and an exercise in lesson planning, or rather re-planning. Many student teachers have found it easier, and more fun, to criticise and improve an existing lesson than to plan everything from scratch. At a more fundamentally important level, Roger Knight's materials in Chapter 6 raise the issues and argument (often deeply felt) about what is 'good English', and what are the teacher's responsibilities in relation to it. Allan Jones and Norma George show that helping pupils whose mother tongue is not English is a task to which every subject teacher can contribute.

Acknowledgments to previous writers on all these topics appear in the appropriate chapters. One of our aims has been to bring together in convenient form material which we have found useful in teacher-training courses, but which has only been available in scattered sources. We cannot claim that these ideas are original, and we have not been aiming to advance the academic study of language, only to help bridge the gap between that and the immediacies of classroom decision-making.

Different ways of using the book

If we are to practise that we preach, it follows that simply to present these ideas, even with illustrative examples, is only a beginning. They have to be appraised by each reader in relation to his or her own experience, modified where necessary and 'brought to life' by examples from many different subjects.

In each chapter, therefore, there is stimulus material for discussion: for example, children's scripts, or extracts from classroom speech, or from textbooks. You are invited to supplement these with your own examples, and to use them as a basis for discussing why some pupils' work is as it is, what are the reasons for setting alternatives, and so on. Each of the main chapters attempts several things:

(a) to introduce ideas *by means of examples,*
(b) to suggest things which a teacher can do, or get pupils to do, in school,
(c) to provide ways of analysing and reflecting upon the resulting information.

Used in that sequence they could form the basis of a college course before, during and after school experience, and that is one of the main ways in which the materials have been used so far. The book is intended to offer a set of systematic enquiries into various aspects of language, that could be carried out by a group as well as an individual. On the other hand, a study group of experienced teachers may find that it is one particular aspect, such as a marking policy, which is of major concern, and the individual chapters are intended to stand on their own.

For beginning teachers the preferred focus is often on the immediate job of how to organise the classroom, rather than on the problematic questions of how children learn. That is one reason why the whole book is closely tied to specific examples. Nevertheless, theoretical ideas about the role of language in learning are always in the background, and that is why they have been spelled out in this introduction. Getting the pupils to make more active use of language in the course of their own learning is likely to be both good for their language development and good for their comprehension of the subject. Hence a fuller awareness of language can, we believe, make a physics teacher a better teacher of physics, not just an extra hand for the English department.

A Caution

Getting pupils to use language well to reflect on their experience, and to extend their own learning, is not just a matter of having a set of techniques. Although we suggest ideas for how to organise writing and discussion, it would be wrong to believe that these will guarantee the desired results. The *context* in which they are used is particularly important: the relationship between teacher and pupil, and the pupil's understanding of how he learns. For example, discussion will occur only in proportion to the amount of trust that exists in the classroom. In developing that trust many factors are involved, but particularly the teacher's own skill as a listener, and the manner in which the learners' contributions are received. Writing too will not grow into a genuine exploration of ideas by the pupil in the absence of an appropriate relationship between the teacher and the pupil. A key feature of this relationship is probably the teacher's willingness and skill in attending to the person behind the writing and talking.

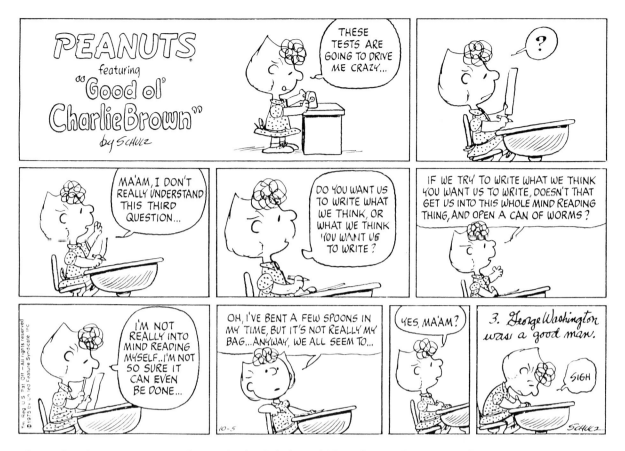

1 Writing: How it is Received

Peter Benton

This chapter is about the ways in which teachers respond to what pupils write. It asks how we come to make certain judgments about our pupils' writing, and asks you to consider what we do with it. In so doing it inevitably opens up much wider considerations about the nature of school learning, the curriculum, and the role of the teacher. The teacher's response to a piece of written work begs the question 'Why was it set in the first place?'. We do not respond in a vacuum and, in that the nature of the question determines the answer, this chapter shoud be read in conjunction with the next, about why and how work may be set. Although the chapter can simply be read through by one person working alone, it might most profitably be used as source material for discussion in a group, preferably a group that includes teachers of several different subjects.

The chapter is in four parts, providing:

(a) some marked scripts for you to discuss,
(b) information about how the pupils feel when they get their scripts back,
(c) some further scripts for you to respond to yourself,
(d) some questions about school policies, and how different schools tackle this problem.

Response to written work matters: it is a main point of contact between teacher and pupil, can be crucial in shaping their relationship, and its impor-

Panel 1.1 *Scripts A and B. What response do you think appropriate? Make whatever assumptions you think reasonable about the background and circumstances. You can find out what the teachers actually wrote by turning to page 28.*

My father is on the broad side and tall side. My father was a hard working man and he had a lot of money. He was not fat or thin... His age was about thirty years when he died, he had a good reputation, he is a married man. When he was in hospital I went to see him every Sunday afternoon. I asked him how he was going on, he told me he was getting a lot better. My father was kind to me and gave me and my cousins cigarette cards. He likes doing woodwork, my father, for me, and he likes a little game of cards now and then; or a game of darts. He chops the wood and saws the planks and he is a handsome man, but he is dead. He worked at the rubber works before he died.

I fetched a bucket of soil and a cup. A jar of sand and some chalk. I fetched a wormery glass which you can see through. I made layers of soil then sand and powdered chalk. I continued like that. Then I put some water in it. I have marked in biro where the water ran. Then I placed four worms in to the wormery. They did not stir when they were on the top of the soil but later they will. I put the wormery into a dark cupboard which is closed.

Discussion of marked scripts

(a) *How effective do you think the marks, comments or corrections might have been in helping the pupil improve his or her writing, and understand more clearly?*

(b) *What criteria seem to be uppermost in each marker's mind?*

(c) *Some markers have a clear view of the kind of language appropriate to their subject. What are your views about this?*

(d) *How important is competence in the technicalities of writing, e.g. spelling and punctuation?*

Note: These are not children you teach, and so you have to make what intelligent guesses you can about the circumstances. One of the potential values of a simulation like this is in comparing your assumptions with those of other teachers. If they were your pupils, what else would you want to know? What do your conclusions suggest about your own policy toward pupils' writing?

tance is often underestimated. There is at least a grain of truth in the contention that the greatest indictment of the whole system is that we spend more time marking than preparing work, but this is not to suggest that marking has no value. As the Bullock Report[1] said: 'Assessment is not in question; it is when it becomes an automatic and unvaried process that it loses its value for both teacher and pupil.'

But what exactly are we assessing, and why? What are the subtle distinctions between terms such as responding, marking, evaluating and assessing? Looking at some written work and some teachers' comments may help focus discussion. On the next few pages you will find several examples of pupils' writing with comments by the teachers (Panels 1.1 to 1.4).

Panel 1.2 *Script C. This was written at home by an eleven-year-old girl, three weeks after joining her secondary school, as an introduction to a topic on 'Birds'. The alteration and correction was in this case done by her father. The part shown here is approximately one third of the total script. The next piece produced by this girl consisted of four sides painstakingly copied verbatim from a fulsome and very difficult book on ornithology.*

Birds

There are all kinds of birds
around. There are ~~big~~ large birds and ~~little~~ small birds
all over the world. The smallest bird
in the world is the humming bird.
~~birds like trees any away Some do.~~
Birds ~~could~~ can be found near ponds,
rivers, and seas. ~~They also like to go~~
~~on land has well.~~ In winter
some of our birds in Britain go away
to other countries. This is called migration
~~from are countrys. was time also~~
~~cotes. All birds builds~~ build ~~their nests~~
~~not the same has each other but~~
~~away that other birds don't know~~
~~a nest is build by grass, hay,~~
~~mud, sometime stone. some birds~~
~~like shining~~ shiny ~~bits of rock, or~~ ~~chocolate~~ chocolate
~~wrapper. Some birds eggs will be~~
~~in their nests.~~

Panel 1.3 *Script D. The author is a boy in the third year in a comprehensive school. The teacher's response is shown on the opposite page.*

The Interrogation

"come, come, Now Jackson Shorly ~~Sorty~~ you now were Frinton street, is", "NO! I Dont", its the Road Next to the River oh' that frinton street NO I was Not in frinton I was at the Disco, oh' No you was not, you were in a house in frinton steet, Robbing Number 46, we have Proth your frend John saw you so, what have you got to say about that. No 1 was at the DISCO, who whit then I cant Rememder. Now. then were is the stuff were DID you put it, ~~woot~~ "what stuff!" Jackson shouted, the 10 grand stall from the suth and you most thave had help from some one else, then the sargent ~~cg~~ come in constable the Results of the finger prints ~~Took~~ Jackson's Dont mach. look. good Lord, thay Dont

If you read this aloud, Robert, it would sound tremendous. (It would make a very good tape.) You have made lots of mistakes though, haven't you?

Try writing it again, looking for these three points :-

"No, I don't."

A new line for each new speaker

"It's the road next to the river."

"Oh, that Frinton Street. No I was not in Frinton Street."

"Where did you put it?"

"What stuff?"

A question mark at the end of a question.

A full stop at the end of each sentence.

How does the story end?

Panel 1.4 *Some contrasting comments as they appeared on teachers' notebooks.*

Teacher's comments on a 13-year old's essays in history:

10/20 *Spelling atrocious*
12/20 *Watch your tenses, but getting better.*
 4/20 *Go through this work and put it into the PAST TENSE.*
 4/20 *Do your spelling corrections. Very poor work.*

Comments written by a geography teacher in the notebooks of 14-year old pupils:

You work quickly, and I'm very pleased with this and with your interest. Do try now to be neater, especially in your diagrams; this would increase your marks. Effort B+. Standard C.

You explain your plans well, and are self critical in a constructive way in the last section. Good summary of Newcastle's actual plans. (Sect.3) Excellent presentation. Standard B+.

A comment at the end of a story about a fox, written by a 15-year old. The actual script contains a consistent misuse of the apostrophe s, all ringed by the teacher in red ink.

C. I'm not v. impressed. Your work is MEDIOCRE, lacking real control and care. You will force me to take the matter up with other staff unless you produce work of a higher quality.

Panel 1.5 *Some learners' recollections on how their work was marked.*

'I mean you write it down to show the teacher that you've done it but it doesn't bring out any more knowledge in you, I don't think. Well, just getting a piece of paper, saying, oh, I'll write all this down, you know, and just to show the teacher you've done it and he just ticks it and you've done that bit of work.'

David, aged 13

At secondary school it was always writing to please whichever teacher was taking you. The fifth form was the worst for writing essays — due to the teacher we had. They all had to be very interesting to him otherwise they were no good....'

College student

'My first notion of the change in emphasis between junior and grammar school came when I had to write an essay on Neolithic man for my first piece of history homework. I started 'My name is Wanda and I am the son of the headman in our village.' The history master read it out to the rest of the class in a sarcastic voice — everybody laughed and I felt deeply humiliated. I got 3/20 for covering the page with writing. I hated history after that until the third year.'

College student

'As soon as we get our books back there's a great "What did you get?... I got so and so." If you mark people low they get very discouraged and people do care about their marks. If you get an E it's quite a nasty punishment and we have one teacher who says things like 'Somebody who shall remain nameless let our form down by getting only 3 out of 10.' Of course everyone knows who it is. Why *do* teachers get us to call out our marks instead of putting them in a book while marking them?'

Nicholas, aged 11

Possible approaches

What options are open to a teacher faced with thirty pieces of work ready for marking? He could:

(a) go through each meticulously correcting all errors of grammar, spelling and punctuation,
(b) be selective in choosing particular errors,
(c) correct misunderstanding or mistakes of content,
(d) give a mark or grade,
(e) add a written comment,
(f) make a note in his mark book of particular problems,
(g) suggest/require corrections to be done,
(h) go over areas of common difficulty with the whole class,
(i) read out particular pieces,
(j) see individual pupils about their work,
(k) 'publish' the work in some way — e.g. place a copy on display,
(l) simply put a tick to indicate that it has been read,
(m) use it as the basis for further work,

and so on. Or perhaps his response might be a combination of two or three of these.

What a teacher does will be determined in part by the intention underlying the specific piece of work set, within the larger context of his perception of the teacher's role. Consider, for example, the following extract from a fifteen-year-old pupil's geography book:

An erratic is quite an exciting result of glaciation as a large rock not geologically the same as its surroundings may be found perched incredibly precariously on smaller stones. This is an erratic.

His teacher has put a red ring round 'exciting' and written in the margin 'No need to get excited. "Spectacular " a better word to use here.' About this response Harold Rosen writes:

Every need to get excited one would have thought; excitement about erratics cannot be so abundant that teachers can afford to dampen it. At least the teacher is showing some concern for language, for the language of his subject, even if his concern is misplaced. How far has his concern taken him? Has he really worked out the nature of definition and what kind of difficulty the pupil, using his own language, had in attempting the task? What is 'better' about 'spectacular' and 'worse' about 'exciting'? Perhaps he is pedagogically wrong and linguistically right. He knows, at least intuitively, that in adult scientific use 'exciting' would find no place in the definition of an erratic; this is his intuitive linguistic criterion. 'Exciting' brings to the definition personal, idiosyncratic, subjective aspects of an erratic which the recording scientist sets out to eliminate. An erratic is an erratic whether you get excited about it or not. To grasp fully what an erratic is you may indeed need to get excited about it, however mildly, but when you have learnt to distinguish between your excitement and the objective properties of the erratic, you have reached a stage when you know something about your own thinking. Thus there is also a psychological criterion of linguistic difficulty.[2]

Making knowledge one's own may *require* excitement over an erratic; it may require personal anecdote, and certainly requires the chance to formulate and reformulate ideas in a supportive and non-threatening atmosphere where expressive language is not only acceptable but encouraged. Michael Polanyi, himself a scientist successful in handling 'objective' knowledge, writes: 'The ideal of a Knowledge embodied in strictly impersonal statements now appears self-contradictory, meaningless, a fit subject for ridicule. We must learn to accept ... a knowledge that is manifestly personal.'[3] Yet often the teacher's response to a pupil's work is bent on rooting out the personal, chivvying him towards a world of 'objective' depersonalised language which, though it has its place, does not always meet present need.

The impact on the learner

Reading what children have to say about the way in which their written work is received (Panel 1.5), one cannot help but pick up the same refrains over and over again. The teacher is often seen as 'judge, jury and hangman',[4] for much of the time perceived as 'Examiner' rather than a trusted adult, and it is overwhelmingly the case that most pupils see the teacher as the person for whom they write. The survey undertaken by the Writing Across the Curriculum Project[5] suggests that around 90 percent of writing in school is written for the teacher and over half of that for the teacher construed as an examiner. Further, outside English and religious education, writing for the teacher as examiner rarely falls below 70 percent. Around two-thirds of writing in school is concerned with classifying particulars — four times as much as any informative writing, twice as much as any 'artistic' writing, and eight times as much as any expressive or speculative writing. In general, their research indicates that the range of types of writing allowed and encouraged is small, particularly in certain subjects, and that the perception of audience is largely teacher-dominated.

In Barnes' terms, most writing in school still seems to fall into the 'transmission' category,[6] where the teacher sees its purpose primarily as the acquisition or recording of information. Here, when the teacher set the work, he thought mainly of the *product* — the kind of writing he hoped his pupils would do — and of whether the task was appropriate and clear. He saw marking primarily in terms of *assessment* and either handed back the written work with no follow up, or used it as a basis for the correction of errors. (A teacher whose approach emphasises the interpretative use of language would see the purpose of writing either in terms of the cognitive development of the writer, or more generally as aiding his or her personal development.) In setting the work he would be concerned with pupils' attitudes to the task, and aware of aspects of the context in which the writing is to be done, such as the audience to be addressed and the range of choices available. He would see marking primarily in terms of making replies and comments, and would be concerned to publish his pupils' work by various means, and to use it as the basis of future teaching.

You may find it helpful to read the whole of the relevant passage in Douglas Barnes's book and, in this context, ask yourself how far a teacher's attitude and approach to marking work is indicative of and shaped by the way he views himself and what we customarily call 'knowledge'. Consider too, Sally's dilemma in the 'Peanuts' cartoon strip (p.7)[7]. The teacher is the audience for whom she writes. Should she write according to her personal perception of George Washington, or should she aim at reproducing something approximating the accepted form of words transmitted by the teacher? Our rueful smile is one of recognition. There is no real choice, and we recognise that the teacher's response is intimately bound up with his intention and that, in general, educational success is measured by the degree of conformity to school values. Pete McGuire and Susie Daniels make this point when they quote the following from a member of an East End gang:

> I like getting 'this is good' because it is a compliment on your work, I don't like it when they start to have a go at you. When I did my stuff on animals, they would always have a different opinion than me, because I don't like pretty birds, ya know, I like things like eagles and vultures, ya know what I mean and they used to say 'Why haven't you got the bird of paradise in it?' ... well I don't like the fucking 'orrible things![8]

Allied to this pressure for some kind of conformity in content there is often a concentration on surface features of the writing to such an extent that it is easy to find marking becoming a kind of solemn game where the teacher feels secure and, in the knowledge that by exchanging the work for a number and the correction of technical errors, he is clearly 'teaching' and they must perforce be learning. The limitations of this approach are soon apparent to the participants, though for either side to break away from its rules is not always easy. On the purely practical level, a teacher who has learned to scan pieces for 'mistakes' without actually reading can at least keep up a brave pretence of being aware of what his pupils write. In general the deception does not work for long, and some pupils will react with hostility to an unreal situation where what they consider to be real effort on their part has gone unappreciated:

> When I get a piece of work back and I think it is good and I get a bad mark I feel like frotiling the teacher.
>
> *Boy aged 14*

This may seem rather drastic, but consider for a moment:

(a) What are your feelings about the marking of your own work by your tutors in recent years? What approaches are most/least helpful? Is there anything you particularly dislike?

(b) Do you remember from your own schooldays a piece of work with which you were particularly pleased and where the response from the teacher seemed inappropriate?

(c) Looking back over the various comments by pupils about the marking of written work, do you find that any of them echo your own experiences, whether as a pupil or as a student-teacher?

(d) How do *you* react to spelling mistakes, ungrammatical usage, incorrect punctuation, and so on? Some teachers express great annoyance when faced with these problems. Why is this?

(e) According to the Schools Council Project, the teacher 'becomes an audience on whom the pupils must focus a special kind of scrutiny in order to detect what they must do to satisfy him.'[5]

Discussion of unmarked scripts

In the light of your discussion and reactions so far, it may now be useful to tackle some unmarked pieces (Panels 1.6 to 1.13). If possible, discuss your response to them in an interdisciplinary group, for then criteria which might be taken for granted by a single subject group are more likely to be challenged. Preferably each subject specialist should hear what others have to say before giving his own response to a script in his own subject. Then consider:

(a) How far are you agreed on what is a 'good' piece of writing and what is not? What factors did you take into consideration?

(b) What are the special problems facing teachers in different subject areas?

(c) Where appropriate, what strategies might be adopted to improve performance?

Panel 1.6 *A poem by a fourteen-year-old girl who has a speech defect.*

My mind
Knows the words,
My mouth and lungs begin
To sound the sentence —
   B - B - BLOCKAGE.

Tight
No breath
No stop-sto-st-ss
FINISH.

And then
     Expecting blockage:

One word free,
Linked to next
And next...
     Steady stream of
   Words,
    Calm,
     Clear,
      Sentence
    After sentence.
And I can talk, talk, talk, talk, talk...

Yet no-one notices.

Panel 1.7 *Part of a chemistry homework by a girl aged fifteen in response to the question: How is a liquid like, or not like, a football crowd? Another script from the same class is shown on the next page.*

Why is a liquid like, or not like, a football crowd.

First of all, the kinetic theory suggests that all matter is made up of tiny particles called molecules, which are always in continuous motion. Fans, off course, are always like this, all being small bits of one big crowd and they never stay still at a game.

Also, liquids take the shape of their container; put a football crowd in a hexagonal stand, and they will take on that shape.

When the liquids temperature is increased, the particles vibrate even more fiercely and eventually those erotic movements overcome the internal attractive forces and the particles in the liquid break away i.e. the liquid boils Likewise, when trouble begins to bubble at a match, the fans blood begins to boil and they start to move about even more. ~~Finally, they~~ Eventually, they break away and spill out onto the pitch.

However, on cooling, the particles slow down and come back to their principle state. The same thing happens at the match, when the trouble dies down, the fans go back to their seats.

They flow in through the gates into the staduim, which can be compared with the containing vessel.

~~Seo~~ Secondly they all sit together, like in a liquid which will assume the shape of the vessel as much as it can, and can only take up a certain volume, like a small crowd can only take up a certain volume. It can also be argued howerever that if one compares each person as a molecule a crowd is not at all like a liqiud since the crowd can be evenly dispersed thus seeming to use up all the stadium, like a gas. However the crowds seem to join together in a close group, thus a crowd is more like a liquid. Also as in a liquid this bunch does not have any specific shape.

Is one would also compare a liqiud is a crowd and heat it, the actual match! being the source of heat, then the molecules, compared to people would start to vibrate.

Panel 1.8 *Two experiences of science lessons written by twelve-year-olds. Anna's recollections were written at home and then taken in for her chemistry teacher. Julie's poem records another aspect of how it feels to be in a laboratory.*

Today we did an experiment where we heated substances. We had a lot of funny results like the Magnesium. When we put that in the flame of the bunsen burner it flared up bright for about six seconds and then dies down. It was a metal when we put it into the flame but after it flares up it is just bits of white on the asbestos sheet. There were two other funny ones, they were Ammonium chloride (which I got in my cut) and copper. The copper one was a bit of copper in a test tube that had to be heated. (Amanda left the tube in the flame to long so the tube began to melt). The copper went black. When it was nearly cool the black stuff began to peel itself off. Underneath there was just a bright orange/red colour. The Ammonium chloride was a white powder in a test tube. When it was heated it made a white vapour up the top of tube. When it was cool the white marks were still on the test tube. We did some other experiments like, Copper carbonate, Cobalt chloride and copper sulphate. These results were not as good so I won't tell you about them.

Anna.

The Science Laboratory
It's a dull Summer morning,
The lights are on,
I feel tired and worn out,
The aparatus is twinkling dully in
the false light,
Although the Bunsens are on I feel
cold,
The Smells of chemicals make me
shiver
Everyone is talking and I feel astho-
ug I am in a world of my own.

Julie

Panel 1.9 *A poem by Colin, aged seventeen.*

DISSECTION

This rat looks like it is made of marzipan
Soft and neatly packaged in its envelope;
I shake it free.
Fingering the damp, yellow fur, I know
That this first touch is far the worst.
    There is a book about it that contains
Everything on a rat, with diagrams,
Meticulous, but free from blood
Or all the yellow juices
I will have to pour away.
    Now peg it out:
My pins are twisted and the board is hard
But, using force and fracturing its legs
I manage though
And crucify my rat.
    From the crutch to the throat the fur is
    ripped
Not neatly, not as shown in the diagrams,
But raggedly,
My hacking has revealed the body wall
As a sack that is fat with innards to be torn
By the inquisitive eye
And the hand that strips aside.
    Inside this taut, elastic sack is a surprise;
Not the chaos I had thought to find,
No oozing mash; instead of that
A firmly coiled discipline
Of overlapping liver, folded gut;
A neatness that is like a small machine—
And I wonder what it is that has left this rat
Why a month of probing could not make it go
    again
What it is that has disappeared ...
    The bell has gone, it is time to go for lunch.
I fold the rat, replace it in its bag
Wash from my hands the sweet
Smell of meat and formalin
And go and eat a meat pie afterwards.
    So, for four weeks or so I am told
I shall continue to dissect this rat.
Like a child
Pulling apart a clock he cannot mend.

Panel 1.10 *The author, Kevin, is aged eleven.*

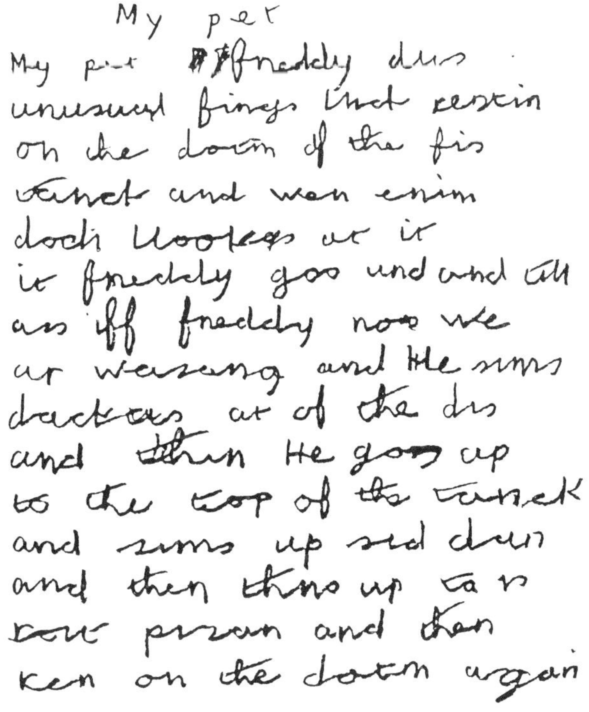

My pet
My pet Freddie does
unusual things like resting
on the bottom of the fish
tank and when any
body looks at it
Freddy goes under and it's
as if Freddy knows we
are watching and he swims
backwards out of the dish
and then he goes up
to the top of the tank
and swims upside down
and then turns up to this
rude (?) person and then
comes on the bottom again.

Panel 1.11 *The author is a girl aged about fourteen. The original script was written on two sides of paper. Here it is condensed by typing, but her alterations and crossings-out are included as they were in the original.*

<u>Conflict</u>

Nag, nag, nag, nag, nag. Always the same.

"Come on, Anne, get changed. We~~d~~'re going in ten minutes."

"What shall I wear?"

"Oh, I don't ~~d~~ know. How about your red outfit?"

"I wore that last time. Anyway, its in the wash."

On and on. Getting crosser and crosser. Not getting anywhere.

"We should have been there five minutes ago. If you don't put your skirt on at once,I'll ~~g~~ come and wallop you!"

"O.K., I'll put it on. But my blouse is in the wash.

She hits me. I hit her back. We ~~swore~~ swear at each other. Then Dad joined in.

"Come on, we're late. Get dressed AT ONCE!"

I can't. I haven't got anything to wear."

On and on. Always the same.

Mum ~~rang~~ rings up the people we ~~were~~ are going to see.

"I'm sorry we're late, Mrs Hill. Anne's being difficult."

Showing me up. ~~in front~~ Making me sound like a baby. But it's not ~~al~~ my fault. She ought to buy me more clothes. I've grown out of half of them and the other half are in the wash. Its not fair!

"Why don't you go without me then? I can manage by myself."

"Don't be daft. You can't man~~g~~age. We don't what time we'll be back. Now put your grey dress on!"

On and on. Round and round.

I'm so sore it hurts to move. Exaughsted from crying. So tired I just want to get into bed and fall asleep.

"Alright, I'll put something on if you go away."

But I can't. I haven't got anything to put on. But there's my scruffy brown cords and that green jumper. I can't be bothered to look nice. Wash my face with cold water, put powder and eye-shadow on.

"You look a right mess. Well, we can't wait any longer. Get in the car."

I almost burst out crying again. I don't want to go. It'll be awful.

But we go, and ~~al~~ Mum shows me up again in front of her friends, and makes nasty remarks. And everybody can see I've been crying, and they know why.

And afterwards Mum will sort of apologise.

"We love you really, of course we do."

I outwardly accept her apologies. But I don't th~~e~~ink she's really sorry. She can't be. That means she doesn't love me. I don't think she can. She wouldn't show me up like that if she did. And I cry, more than I did last ~~me~~ night, and I wonder. if she does love me. I don't trust her after last night, she might do anything.

But after a few days I trust her again, because I have to. And we carry on alright until the next big flare-up.

Panel 1.12 *An account from a mathematics lesson, the writer is aged eleven and a half.*

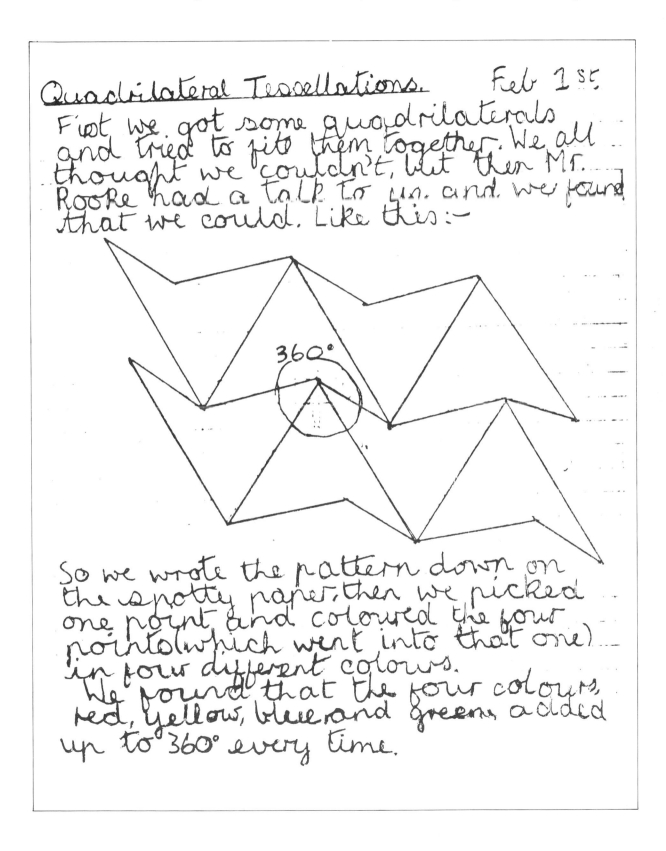

Quadrilateral Tessellations.   Feb 1st

First we got some quadrilaterals and tried to fit them together. We all thought we couldn't, but then Mr. Rooke had a talk to us. and we found that we could. Like this:—

So we wrote the pattern down on the spotty paper, then we picked one point and coloured the four points (which went into that one) in four different colours.

We found that the four colours, red, yellow, blue and green, added up to 360° every time.

Panel 1.13 *Robert's work in four subjects for a complete week. He is aged thirteen and a half.*

IN GEOGRAPHY. The children were asked to use textbooks and information learned in class and to write about industries in California.

Aircraft

The biggest Aircraft company in america is the Northrop corporation trade name Beoing it is based at Beverly hills, California, perhaps the most famous plane they have built is the 707 which was sold to many leading Airlines encluding Saudi Arabian Airlines, Etheopian Airways, Aranca, Continental Western, EL AL, Northwest Orient, Lofthansa, PIA and pan am, Also beoing have had great successes with there 720, 727, 737 and 170 And now there is the 747 Gumbo Jet and the first to carry 500 passangers.

Gold

California was the first gold produsing State in North America and produces one third of American gold the mines are around the foothills of Siera Nevada.

Oil

The oil wells are at the upper end of San Joaqin Valley by Los Angeles. It is pumped to refineries on the coast such as San Franciso, Molney, Portland, Harford, Santa Monica and Wilmington. This oil is exported all over the world.

Filming

California has proved a most convenient place for filming because of the clear skys well lit from the sun ..... (not finished).

IN HISTORY. The pupils were instructed to write an account of some English seamen of the sixteenth century, mentioning the lands they sailed to, the trading they were involved in, the hazards they encountered, and the character of the men themselves.

Some English Seamen of the 16th century

John Hawkins

In 1568 John Hawkins sail the atlantic selling slaves to America. This slaves were captored in africa and take often to america to be sold as cotton workers. Most of them died on the way to there distenation the ones that did not die. Did not last very long the climate was hot and they were not well fed. The pope realised how monsterous this was and band it But John Hawkins being a protistant toke no notice and caried on his trading, this was not to last long for the spanish sunk his ship because of his unloyaty to the pope

Sir W Ralaigh

Started up a settlement in Virginia in 1620 the pilgram farthers fled to Virginia to escape persiation becorce they were puritanes.

IN ENGLISH. Pupils were given photographs taken from magazines and, after discussing their particular picture with a partner, were asked to write firstly an objective description of the picture, then to write about any topic which the picture brought to their minds.

Young children moving in after the demolishion Squad. Siting on bricks roude a fire made in an old cake tray midst the view of broken down walls, ages old cement, crumbold up bricks the dust wizing in the air ful to them a wonderous play ground of games and imagination It was in the summer of 1960 the gas men came down ower street to lay the new gas pipes To do this thay had to dig up the pavment and half the road, as it was hot, All the workmen were striped down to waste. There brown bodyes shone like gold, There miseles bulging as if they would burst as they swing there picks tearing lumps of tar from the road piles of tar lie scatered above masive hands throw the old tar into lorreys

IN CHEMISTRY. This was written immediately after seeing a demonstration of the experiment. There was a blackboard summary: Combination of Oxygen and Hydrogen. Plastic bottle — water, ⅓ full oxygen cylinder, ⅔ full hydrogen — Kipps apparatus, water formed. The class were told to write as they would normally write an experiment in their books.

Cobination of Oxegen and hydrogen

Method. A plastic bottile was filled to the top with water then imersed in a tank of water (tap water) then one third of the bottel was filled with hydrogen which was obtained from a cylinder of hydrogen then the next two thirds were filled with Oxegen got from a Kip which was made by passing Sylveric acid over zinc which forms Oxegen then a lited splint was put to it

Result   A vilent flame and bang aperd

Conclusion   Oxegen and hydrogen explode when a flame is put to it.

IN ENGLISH AGAIN. Most boys have not been in women's hairdressers and vice versa. In mixed groups of 5-6, girls were asked to tell boys about going to the hairdressers and boys to tell girls — concentrating on sensations (feelings, smell, etc.). Back in the whole class, the teacher elicited comments and asked the class to write as vivid an account as possible, boys now writing about men's hairdressers and girls about women's.

As you enter a barbers shop a sweet smell of spray hits you. You sit on a cold hard chair as the sisers click behind the buze of electric clips. The tone changes as the barber puts the clipers to the hair of someone except for that everyone sits in silense. The ocassional flick of a page disterbs this atmosphere. After that about five minuets you get dry in the throt from the fumes from the littel cylindrical oil fire stuck in the corner licking the taste from the air. Then all the buzing stops and a clear Next as you sit sliring into the Mirror for there is nothing else to do the buzzing startes again and you get a titaling sensation runing down your spine from the clipers on your neck. But it is a relif to get out

A school policy

Where teachers have begun to examine the idea of a language policy for the whole school, the methods of response to written work often provide a basis for their early discussions. Panel 1.14 shows headings from the minutes of a staff meeting.[9] If you were taking part in a meeting addressing such questions, what points would you wish to make?

Another concern of teachers, not included in the agenda shown, emerges from correspondence in the columns of the *Times Educational Supplement* which is reproduced in Panel 1.16.[10] If this is the reality for some teachers, and if we do indeed 'applaud and endorse' James Britton's remarks, can we suggest approaches that might help us strike the right balance? A Head of English in a comprehensive school in an industrial village presented the pupils with notes on 'The way your English written work will be marked'[11] (shown in Panel 1.15). Is it one that you could adapt, or indeed would want to adapt, to suit other subject areas?

Having read so far and considered some of the problems posed by responding to what pupils write, are you able to come full circle and do what the teacher who received Script C (p.9) felt she had to do — that is, could you compose a letter to the parent of the girl explaining how you regard marking and advising the parent how best to take an interest in the child's work?

Panel 1.14 *Agenda headings from the minutes of a school staff meeting.*

1 The teacher's written comment at the end of a piece of work.
   (a) What is its purpose? *(b)* Does it matter what tone, and style, it is written in?

2 The marking of errors.
   (a) Which mistakes in spelling, punctuation and expression should be marked?
   (b) In what manner should mistakes be corrected?

3 The marking of accuracy.
   (a) How important is it to mark successful uses of language and accuracy of expression? *(b)* How can we develop a pupil's best work?

4 What part does discussion with a pupil play in the marking of his/her work?

Some possible further enquiries in school

(In the case of a student-teacher these should only be carried out after discussion with your supervising teacher)

(a) Do individual Departments have a policy on marking, and is there any overall school policy?

(b) What would be a typical marking load for a teacher in a particular subject? How long does it take each week to cope with it? What strategies are adopted?

(c) Ask if you may examine the exercise books of one pupil in a given subject over a period of time. What are the comments made? Are they likely to have a cumulative effect? Look back on your own marking and ask the same questions of yourself.

(d) If possible, collect the written work of one pupil over a single week: a photocopy of each piece is ideal. What are the expectations of the teachers in different subjects, and what criteria underlie their marking?

(e) Interview a group of pupils. What do they like and dislike about the way their work is marked? What do they find most and least helpful?

(f) In what ways do teachers keep a working record of each pupil's difficulties and progress? Can you devise a system for doing this yourself? Be realistic about the time it requires of you.

Panel 1.15 *A document given to pupils by English teachers in a comprehensive school.*

The way your English written work will be marked.
(Note: If your parents take an interest in your English and read your work, let them read this too.)

1.   First you must understand that not all your written work in English needs handing in for 'marking'. For instance rough work, where you sort out your ideas on paper for a group play, or for a speech, or for a piece of later neat work, or where you makes notes on a book for later revision; these do not need marking. Such work can be as untidy and 'shorthand' as you like so long as it serves your purpose.

2.   Next, understand that your English teachers will not always judge that the best way to appreciate your work is to give it back covered in red ink. Would you do that to a piece of writing - like this - from the teacher? Sometimes your teacher may simply read your piece with pleasure, or for information, as he would a book.

3.   When your teachers do choose to mark your work, it may not always be to correct or grade it (though they may keep grades, which they do not write on your work, in their mark books, to record your progress). How it is marked depends on what your work is intended to be and who it is intended for. If you tell the teacher, someone you know, about something interesting, you should expect him to reply in the same way, like a penfriend. If you are trying out a way of writing on the teacher, you'd expect to receive help on how to write that way, like a master's advice to an apprentice. If you're writing to prove your competence at something - a test - expect to be told how far you've succeeded (a grade) and where you've gone wrong (correction).

4.   In general, *what* you write or say is more important than *how* you write or say it. So teachers will often discuss what you write rather than the way you write it: they will argue with you or write back. That should flatter you, because it means the teacher is interested, rather than irritated, by what you write.

5.   When they are correcting, teachers won't correct every 'mistake' you make. To start with, the 'how' of what you write is not always as simple as being a matter of right or wrong. There is more than one way of writing something, and which way you choose has to do with what is most appropriate to the context in which you write and to your relationship with the reader.

6.   What to do about marking.
If the teacher starts a discussion provoked by your writing, join in, either in talk or writing. If it's in writing, the teacher would probably prefer that to be your next homework rather than the work he's set to the rest of the class. If the teacher writes questions in your work, answer them in writing: the teacher asks you questions rather than giving you answers, to make you think and learn. If the teacher explains something, note it, or if you don't understand it, ask: you will be expected not to need that explanation again. If the teacher suggests corrections, do them: some things are soonest learnt by intensive practice, and doing such corrections give you practice at what the teacher thinks you should by now be doing conventionally.

Panel 1.16 *(Reproduced by permission)*

No time for marking

Sir, I am enjoying a sabbatical term's leave of absence (the first in 20 years) from the comprehensive school where I am responsible for the English department. This week, as part of my work towards producing a textbook, I came across the following words in *The Development of Writing Abilities* (11-18) - a report by James Britton and others from a five year Schools Council project.

"Very close reading of children's writing is essential, because that is the best means we have of understanding their writing processes. Children value perceptive comments, responses and questions on their writing, but they quickly see through perfunctory approval and general-ized faint praise. And it is worth remembering that for very many children, for many years, their teachers are the only readers of the bulk of their work."

Of course, any experienced teacher who is at all familiar with children's writing would want to applaud and endorse these remarks. But I have also, this week, had the task of allocating staff to classes for 1977-1978 and I would like to measure the admirable words just quoted against the practical realities of my school.

The normal teaching allocation is 35 periods out of 40. As the head of a department of ten I am only required to teach 32 periods. Now, as with many other schools, English as a separate subject starts in the third year. Consequently, an English specialist can expect to teach five or six sets in years 3-4, with some sixth form work; to be more specific, he or she will be responsible for the English teaching of 170-200 pupils, including CSE, 'O' and 'A' level groups.

In order to spend five minutes reading and marking the week's work of each pupil, roughly fifteen hours marking is required. In practice little marking can be achieved in the classroom - perhaps a couple of hours a week. Moreover, the already small number of non-teaching periods is regularly diminished by cover for staff absences or extra coaching or tuition.

The net result is that in order to give, I repeat, five minutes a week to the writing of each pupil, an English teacher needs to spend two to three hours marking for five or six evenings a week. This is in addition to any necessary preparation, meetings after school, parents' evenings, marking examinations, writing reports or, occasionally, personal reading.

I have specified these facts because they are typical of what obtains in many state secondary schools. Most of these teachers will never be granted a sabbatical term. Some, including many excellent, sensitive people who achieve fine results with children, escape from the stresses of the classroom and the incessant slog of marking and preparation into basically administrative posts.

I know of no simple solution; but I do know that it is dishonest and demoralizing to pretend that standards of written expression can be improved or even maintained in our schools while, at the same time, teachers are given larger classes and insufficient time to do their work properly.

R.V. BATEMAN
Jesus College
Cambridge

Sir, Like your correspondent ("No time for marking") I know what it is like to spend "two to three hours marking for five or six evenings a week".

I teach in an English department in which we try to close mark everything pupils write and since we are mixed ability in Years 1 to 4 I fancy that gives us more marking and preparation than with sets.

I think it is about time English teachers considered whether or not they concentrate over much on written work to the extent that oral and aural work is neglected.

What written work that is done should be considered carefully with a view to what pupils actually learn from doing it. It should never be writing just for writing's sake but should be done by pupils with a view to them obtaining carefully defined objectives set by the teacher.

If someone asked me as an English teacher why I work such long hours marking I would say I marked for the satisfaction of seeing pupils respond to what I hope are perceptive comments, responses and questions on their writing.

However, if I am too tired next morning to class teach the next lesson then I'm failing my pupils - for all my labour in marking the night before. The English teacher operates in "the space between" which should be full of the give and take of talk and listening between him and his pupils. In the past there has been perhaps too much writing and too little pupil-teacher interaction.

If we can strike the right balance between writing, listening and talk then perhaps we will give the English teacher more time for marking and, very important, more time for the self-development which should in turn make him a better teacher.

STEWART ROBERTSON
Head of English,
Castell Alun High School,
Hope, Nr Wrexham, Clwyd.

References

1   The Bullock Report, *A Language for Life,* HMSO, 1975.
2   'The Language of School Textbooks', Harold Rosen in *Language in Education,* Routledge and Kegan Paul, 1972.
3   Michael Polanyi, in Hourd, M., *Relationship in Learning,* Heinemann, 1972.
4   Nancy Martin *et al., Writing and Learning Across the Curriculum, 11-16,* Ward Lock, 1976.
5   See *The Development of Writing Abilities 11-18,* James Britton *et al.,* Macmillan, 1975.
6   Douglas Barnes, *From Communication to Curriculum,* Penguin, 1976, pp. 139-58.
7   Peanuts, featuring 'Good Ol' Charlie Brown', by Charles Schulz.
8   McGuire, P., and Daniels, S., (eds), *The Paint House,* Penguin, 1972.
9   The Headmaster and Staff, Bicester School, Oxfordshire.
10 *The Times Educational Supplement,* 27 May and 10 June, 1977.
11 Quoted in Mike Torbe, *Language Across the Curriculum: Guidelines for Schools,* N.A.T.E. in association with Ward Lock, 1976.

Further Reading

Dunsbee, T., and Ford, T., *Mark my Words,* Ward Lock Educational, 1980.

Teachers comments on the scripts in Panel 1.1.
Script A: The teacher wrote: 'Tenses. You keep mixing past and present'.
Script B: The science teacher wrote: 'Not very good, but might be alright in English, creative writing, or something'.

2   *Writing: How it is Set*

Owen Watkins

Nearly all pupils find writing more difficult than speaking, partly of course because they get less practice in everyday life, though it should be remembered that talk may on occasion be hard — when for instance the situation is intimidating, or when it is necessary to think very quickly. But the task in any case imposes formidable constraints. Harold Rosen, in connection with the Writing Across the Curriculum Project, put it this way:

> The writer is a lonely figure cut off from the stimulus and corrective of listeners. He must be a predictor of reactions and act on his predictions. He writes with one hand tied behind his back, being robbed of gesture. He is robbed too of the tone of his voice and the aid of the clues the environment provides. He is condemned to monologue; there is no-one to help out, to fill the silences, put words in his mouth, or make encouraging noises.

However, this isolation could have a positive value if it allows the writer to think through an argument without being interrupted.

Recent studies of what children write in a school week suggest that their assignments are made even *more* difficult than this, possibly because their teachers underestimate how complex the process of mastery is, and/or because they set insufficiently varied tasks. Pupils have been restricted to a narrow range of assignments designed almost exclusively to test what they have learned, and even here they have been left uninformed about many of the contextual factors which in any situation outside school would help them to plan the form, content and style of what they write. Moreover, there seems to be an explicit or implied demand that every piece of work should be in 'final draft' form, using the kind of language found in textbooks. This may rob pupils of the chance to sort out for themselves their own understanding of what they are learning.

So teachers might find it useful to look at the purposes of written work in schools in other ways. Two such approaches are worth considering, and they offer a range of practical suggestions:

(a) Is language being used for the 'transmission' or 'interpretation' of knowledge?

(b) Does the pupils' writing have a clear *function*, and a definite *audience*?

Transmission and Interpretation

Douglas Barnes's distinction between a 'transmission' and an 'interpretation' view of language is set out fully in Chapter 5 of his book *From Communication to Curriculum*. Its importance has already been mentioned in the previous chapter, and it will form the basis of a further study in Chapter 8. Here we are concerned with its effect on what pupils are asked to write. The 'transmission' view assumes that language is simply the medium for communicating ideas from teacher to pupil (or vice versa). The 'interpretation' view implies that pupils have to reinterpret knowledge for themselves in order to possess it, by trying to express it again in their own way. As with any hypothesis involving contrasting concepts, it is important not to apply it too rigidly or to make it explain too much, and most teachers probably make use of both views to some extent, but few would dispute that most written assignments in school presuppose a transmission view. This need not necessarily be so.

Looking for evidence of 'interpretation'

Look at panels 2.1 to 2.4 and/or some scripts collected from your own school. What evidence can you find in them of interpretative activity as the pupils think through what they are writing about?

Panel 2.1 *A history script in which pupils are asked to imagine historical events from the point view of people of the time (from* Ideas for Teaching History, *by Sean Healy).*

To our Respected
Members of Parliament

The people and merchants of Stevenage, a fair town in the County of Hertfordshire, wish to register certain feeble PETITION against the building of certain railways through that town. The objections are:-

1. That the railway will destroy the trade of the town by annihilating the coaching inns and depressing the markets of the town

2. That livestock of the surrounds to the line will be seriously affected, hens will not lay, nor cows proffer milk and animals will be driven crazy by the snorting iron machine

3. That the select township of Stevenage will be impregnated by a race of black-faced, uncouth foulals, attracted by the railways.

4. That the building of the three proposed lines will plough up the countryside RUINING our noble squire, and his neighbouring counterparts, land and livelihood!!

5. That the fumes from the engines will induce chronic disease and ill health and the sparks from the locomotive furnaces will burn the land for miles around, in gigantic FIRES! will burn the land for miles around, in gigantic FIRES!

6. FINALLY that the boilers of the locomotives will blow up, inducing SERIOUS LOSS OF LIFE

Travellers on the Railway will have a SPEEDY TRIP to HELL !!?!

We (the undersigned) therefore PETITION and RESPECTED MEMBERS of the HOUSE of COMMONS to STOP THIS DANGEROUS SCHEME to RUIN our LIVES

SIGNED

D.G. Prescot
D.E.T. (Charger)
ROSY DUKE
Roland Boadman

Tony Millhaven
B wood
Shamus C Heath

Andrew Lee
Alec ? (recently dead)
Well D Gwyn Jr
Bill ('rolling') Jones
Susan Parrett
Mullion ?

Alec Wurzel
← (his mark)

Thomas Thompson (Sg
(SIMPLY) SIMON
Bert Spanner
John
Wayne
← X
(his mark)

Squire Heathcote, of Snephall
Mr. Alexander, town crier
Mr. Dunz, man manure spler
Beach, the village idiot
My Williamson, a pig-breeder
Mr. Wood, the town yard sweeper
Shamus, village scare-(row)
Mr. Lee, publican, the "Roebud"
R.I.P.

Barnaud, the "Roebuck"
Mr. Jones, town guitarist
The Squire's intimate maid
Mr. Crope, osler
Mr. Wurzel CBD, DFO, CDN
Farm Labourer
(Champion Beer-Drinker)
Mr. Thompson, poet (of sorts)
Mr. Simon Something, layabout
Mr. Spanner, car mechanic
Mr. Wayne, cinematography-
performing artiste (time artiste).

Panel 2.2

> The blood defences, it's called. And it's the defence idea I find most interesting, that and the organisation of it all. It's all so military, all of it, and so thoroughly practical. Think of the structure. Invaders appear - bacteria, intent upon their dirty work. Instantly, a signal to the defenders - but how? How do the phagocytes and lymphocytes *recognise* invasion? That's a question I'd like answered. Anyway, they do, somehow, in the mysterious, almost magical way the body has. And then, independent of brain directions, apparently, they move into action.
>
> I like the subtlety of the methods of defence - but of the four, I'm most taken by the simple eating of the bacteria by the phagocytes. The slow, remorseless engulfing of the disease-carrier, while all around the mindless red cells continue their normal activities, completely undisturbed by the death-struggle going on among them - there's an epic quality about it.

Panel 2.3 *After geography lessons on different types of farming in Britain, the teacher set the class the task of examining some aerial pictures and writing descriptions of them. The writer is aged fourteen.*

> Picture A
>
> I)   The main features of farming in this area are large, flat fields of irregular shape. Trees make a wind break and a river and small lake provide water for the land. The land is slightly sloped which allows efficiant draining and a railway provides transport for goods brought in and out of the area.
>
> II)   The type farming is cattle farming, probably dairy cattle because of their colour (black and white - fresions = dairy) although they could possibly be beef cattle. Perhaps in Cheshire
>
> Picture B
>
> I)   The features of this type of farming are flat regular fields with trees lining the field boundaries for wind breaks. Large greenhouses are seen in large block areas and tall chimneys can be seen which would ventilate them. Roads wind through the fields to allow quick and easy transport.
>
> II)   The type of farming is market gardening. The crop seen in the foreground could be raspberries or gooseberries where people might come to 'pick their own'. The field on the far right looks to me to have trees in, possibly apples, plums or pears. The greenhouses could contain tomatoes which can not ripen in the outside where it is colder.

Panel 2.4 *From a mathematics lesson in which the pupils have been studying triangles, and are asked to look for patterns relating the number of triangles with the number of lines needed to draw them. (In this case they have used matchsticks to construct the linked sets of triangles.)*

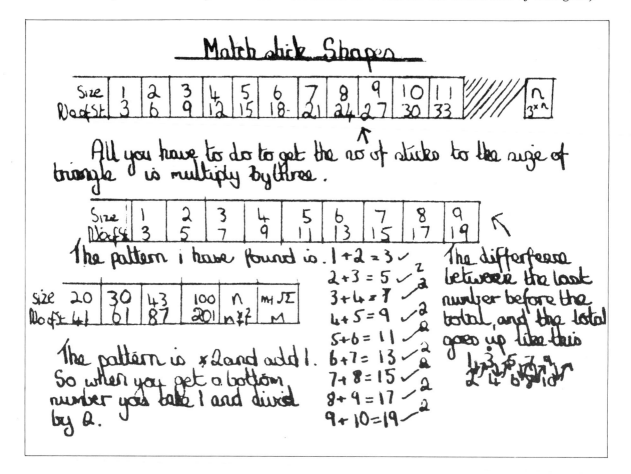

While pupils' writing can and should be used as a medium for feedback to the teacher, the interpretation view almost certainly exploits functions and resources of language more richly, because it obliges the teacher to take into account the features that determine the content and form of a written communication, for example:

WHO says WHAT, to WHOM, and WHY,
and UNDER WHAT CIRCUMSTANCES?

This should result in tasks that are more clearly focused and more varied — for instance, the teacher becomes concerned to encourage intermediate and exploratory writing (i.e. in tentative and draft form) which it is hoped will progressively bridge the gap between pupils' everyday language and that of the subject specialist.

The following two assignments illustrate the differing demands that might be made by history teachers whose views of language contrast in the way just described:

(a) Describe the reformation of hospital nursing brought about by Florence Nightingale.

(b) Write an imaginary extract from Florence Nightingale's diary in 1846, in which she considers whether she should persist in her attempt to start training as a nurse.

Both assignments can be justified, and the same teacher might set both at different times. They fulfil different functions: the second one is not so comprehensive as the first, but to do it the pupil would need to find out about nurses and nursing in the 1840s, and would have to *interpret* this information. The outcome should be a deeper understanding of the situation and of Florence Nightingale's problems at the time; putting it crudely, less may be learnt, but what is learnt is likely to be more meaningful and thus a better basis for further learning. How do you think the sorts of understanding developed in the two assignments differ?

The writer's sense of purpose

Another approach to children's writing was developed by the team of the Schools Council project on 'Writing Across the Curriculum', referred to here as the London Writing Project (see the bibliography, p.46). They suggested that one should look at the *function* of the writing and its *audience*. In respect of function they suggested there are three kinds of writing, which they called 'Expressive', 'Transactional' and 'Poetic'. These differ in the sorts of things the writer takes for granted about his reader's response.

In 'expressive' writing it is taken for granted, they suggested, that *the writer himself* is of interest to the reader; personal letters and diaries are the most obvious forms of expressive writing. It may have little or no conscious structure, but reflects the ebb and flow of the writer's thoughts and feelings. Anna's account of her work in chemistry (Panel 1.8 p.18) might be classified as expressive writing. Her memories, reactions and feelings are all mingled with the factual information as she puts down her first thoughts.

An example of an assignment which might encourage such writing is this: Describe your thoughts and feelings while you consider the prospect of doing something unpleasant but inevitable (for example, apologising to a neighbour for forgetting to deliver an important message; telling your mother you have broken her most valued ornament; admitting having told a lie to someone whose opinion you respect).

In 'transactional' writing on the other hand, it is taken for granted that the writer can be challenged

Transactional? Poetic? Expressive?

"There's a comforting glow in the shop, and cool, satisfying smoke is billowing out of the windows."

After Baxter, reproduced by permission of the Daily Express.

Looking at scripts in term of audience and function

Examine the scripts in Panels 2.5 to 2.9, or others you have collected.

What is your impression of the writer's sense of audience? How far has the teacher helped to develop that sense of audience, and therefore the real communication, by the type of task and how it was set?

	Name of script	*Comments*
Self		
Trusted adult		
Teacher as partner		
Teacher in special relationship		
Teacher as examiner		
Peer group		
Known public		
Unknown public		

Drawing also on other ideas discussed so far, to what extent do you think these scripts have features which could be described as 'expressive' (relatively unshaped first reactions of the writer to his topic), 'transactional' (considered logical statements), or 'poetic' (a statement so polished as to be an art object in itself)?

for its logicality and its *truthfulness to public knowledge;* it is the language for the presentation of facts, for reporting, arguing, persuading and theorising. Examples: *(a)* Describe the manufacture of steel by the Bessemer process; *(b)* Argue the case for allowing only one breadwinner per household in a country where unemployment is rising.

A third category they called 'poetic' writing, in which they said it is taken for granted that *'true or false' is not a relevant question at the literal level.* Rather it is the experience of what is presented that

is significant. This is the language of fiction and poetry; the form is inseparable from the content, and is an essential component of the experience. (It must be said that 'poetic' hardly seems an appropriate term, although 'imaginative' — an obvious alternative — might be thought to deny any imaginative element in 'expressive' or 'transactional' writing.) An example: Write a dialogue that takes place between three people, strangers to one another, who are waiting in a deserted street on a Saturday night for the last bus, which is already ten

Panel 2.5

It makes you feel a bit sick doesn't it at first just talking and thinking about your inside, all modgy and ugh. I mean you look allright from the outside it hard to think that inside you're like that. But that's me inside I wonder what we'd look like without the outside bit? but we couldn't hold together without skin, could we? All those things though, white blood corpuscles and red ones and bacteria, I can't really imagine that they're inside me now, this very minute. I've got a little cut on my finger and there's just a tiny speck of blood there, I can't see how all those many cells and things can be swimming about in that little speck. And those bacteria, they must look horrible, fancy having live things under your skin. Its hard to believe and I can't imagine it at all, they must be so very tiny, white blood cells as well on guard duty ready to get rid of the bacteria, can it really be happening now in me? Perhaps while I'm writing this there's a little battle going on somewhere perhaps in that cut on my finger, I wonder if they know what they're doing, or if they think about it. You tend to think of them as charators don't you? with human chactoristics.

Panel 2.6

I remember well my first visit to G..... hospital. It was a dull afternoon in September, cold but crisp. C...., a teacher, took us to the hospital. We were laughing and joking all the journey, perhaps we wished to hide how nervous we were deep inside. The main building is a big house. A long driveway down to the house is surrounded by trees. It looked like something out of a film set. You wouldn't know the occupants were hundreds of mentally ill people.
Eventually arriving, we walked round the grounds with C..... meeting and chatting to various patients that were walking or keeping themselves busy. We visited the children's ward. A little boy sat outside on the slabs and watched us attentively, not responding to our smiles. I remember that terrible smell in the children's ward. They were in rooms and rushed to the glass door as we approached and pressed their faces against it. Some just sat there in corners and others didn't even notice us.

Panel 2.7

Things I have noticed about a candle

1. It gives light.
2. If the flame is kept still it will stand up straight.
3. It gives a flame like the bunsen burner with the air hole closed but the flame on the candle is more still.
4. It has four different colours in the flame. Blue at the bottom on the wick, dark orange above the blue, yellow in the middle with a faint orange line going through the yellow, then at the top it goes orange.
5. The wax gets to the flame because the wick soaks up the wax, so if you light it you will get a flame.
6. At the top there is a wax liquid.
7. Some of the wax has turned into a gas.
8. When you blow out a candle it gives out smoke and a burning smell.
9. When it burns wax pours down the side and goes hard.
10. As the wick burns it turns into a black cord.

Panel 2.8 *An extract from a pupil's log book in 'Enquiry' lessons in the humanities. The teacher has attempted to get the pupils to enter into a dialogue with him. Andrew is thirteen.*

Andrew: One thing I didn't like about the Industrial Revolution when it came, was the employing of children in factories. They were given dangerous jobs like going under the machines which were in motion. And children which had to work in the coal mines I feel bad about this because when they worked they never went to school and so they grew up they weren't able to read or write. I learn things and am able to write about a certain subject by reading a book or if the teacher reads it out aloud. I myself do a lot of reading at home, but since we got a television I don't do as much as I would like to. I have got an interest in writing plays, I have written two already and acted them with the help of a few friends and a tape. I think it's because of the challenge of writing a good one that makes me interested in them.

Teacher: How could you bring your thoughts about the Industrial Revolution and your interest in playwriting together?

Andrew: A good question, I suppose I could write a play of something out of the industrial Revolution like children working in factories, or about a group of them who try and runaway because they are so fed up with the misery of working in the factory. Or even children who are working in the coal mines. I think that would be a good way of bringing the two subjects together, although it would take a lot of work on my part I should think, because I would have to create the right atmosphere of it and sense what the children feel. Anyway, now it.....

Panel 2.9 *A third-year physics class were taken by a teacher who encouraged them to write their main work just on the right-hand pages. The left-hand pages were to be used for them to write their questions and queries about points they found difficult, or comments on how they felt about the work they had done, as well as for his own answers to these queries. In this case the homework involved writing about the magnetic field of the earth. The script shown here was included by the pupil on a separate piece of paper tucked into the exercise book.*

Sir,
I found this writing in one of my books, but do not understand it and do not know whether to put it in my book or not.
As magma rises along the mid-oceanic ridges from the mantle, iron minerals are lined up with the Earth's magnetic field. Periodically the magnetism is reversed. On magnetic charts of rocks near the ridges, there is a zebra-like pattern of normally magnetized rocks and reverse-magnetized rocks. The pattern is the same on both sides of the ridges because the new rock is divided evenly and moved in opposite directions.

Thank you for writing this out for me. If you don't understand it then don't put it in your book until you know what it is about. Please keep this. When I take the lesson again next week, I shall explain what this means if you remind me, and then you can add it to your notes.

minutes late. The project reports postulate that expressive writing may be basic in the process of trying out and coming to terms with new ideas. If teachers only set 'transactional' writing, then what is learnt could tend not to be related to the learner's existing knowledge, thoughts and feelings. On the other hand, 'transactional' writing, among other things, promotes lucid and orderly handling of information, ideas and thought processes, and we need to know how it can be made to grow, perhaps, out of more personal writing.

A difficulty arises with these categories because they are not mutually exclusive; indeed, three assessors examining over two thousand scripts for the project could agree on the function of fewer than one-third of them. Nevertheless, the ideas behind the categorisation have been found helpful by many teachers. When setting written work we can use the categories, applied to our satisfaction, to help us vary the modes of writing required of pupils over the course of a term or a year, and learn to consider what kinds of learning they appear to promote.

The writer's sense of audience

A second problem with much school writing, the Project team argued, is that it is unreal because it is almost invariably produced for one reader only — the teacher — and it consists of telling him what he already knows. The pupil knows that he knows and that the only purpose of the writing is to enable the teacher to make an assessment of what is said and how it is said, consequently the writing is not a genuine piece of communication. If, however, we vary the kind of audience, identify who the reader is to be, and try to make every piece of work fulfil some genuine communicative purpose, the pupils are likely to do better because they are motivated to write, and clearer about the situation. In the process they will also be obliged to practise a wider range of skills. Possible audiences for school-based writing are:

(a) the writer himself,
(b) a trusted adult (probably the teacher),
(c) the teacher as partner in a dialogue (a personal relationship),
(d) the teacher in a particular pedagogic relationship (e.g. apprentice/master),
(e) the teacher as examiner,
(f) a peer group,
(g) some clearly defined section of the public,
(h) the anonymous public at large.

Getting ready to write

Teachers of English are very aware of the need to encourage pupils' motivation with stimulating ideas and activities. Writing in other subjects is also likely to improve greatly if more attention is given to careful preparatory work.

The teacher's role in this lies partly in stimulating the pupils' imagination through his or her own interest in the subject, and partly in clarifying the purpose of the task and defining possible audiences for the writing. The pupils, for their part, will need to talk out this purpose before the writing ever begins, to exchange ideas and explore possibilities for what to put in it.

The teacher can offer many alternative forms of writing: a dialogue, perhaps, or a TV script, a narrative, or any of the forms encountered in journalism: letters to an editor, editorials, profiles of people, news stories with headlines, crime reports, obituaries, reviews. Imitating one of these models can provide support to the writer. Trying to adopt the style of a well-known broadcast programme or newspaper can also bring variety and enjoyment to writing as well as obliging the writer to look very closely at both his model and the content. If the first priority in teaching is that the process should be enjoyable, there is every ground for trying to ensure that the effort entailed in writing brings as much satisfaction and enjoyment as possible. So humour, satire, parody, diatribe, need not be ruled out as contributions to the understanding of serious and respectable subject disciplines. *Almost any piece of writing that brings enjoyment is likely to increase pupils' engagement with subsequent assignments, especially if the result is shared with others.*

Perhaps more attention has been given to ways of stimulating children's writing than to the early stages of the writing itself. Discussion of first drafts, either with individuals or through a group discussion of examples on an overhead projector, could foster the practice of self-criticsm. That involves learning to ask questions about how well the sequencing, vocabulary, and phrasing contribute to the writer's purpose. 'The difficulty of literature', said Robert Louis Stevenson, 'is not to write, but to

Planning written assignments

Here are some topics from different subjects. Choose one, or a topic which you are currently teaching, and devise several different written assignments for the pupils:

(a) Trial by jury
(b) Industrial relations
(c) Contamination of food in shops and restaurants
(d) Glaciation
(e) Ways of fastening things together
(f) The French attitude to politics
(g) The use of graphs
(h) Science and crime detection
(i) The life of Cleopatra, or Columbus, or Paul of Tarsus, or Winston Churchill, or Charles Dickens or Charles Darwin.

Here are some more ideas for forms of words to use:

'Imagine you are a newspaper reporter who has 500 words to explain this to the readers ....'
'Draft a circular to people whom you want to inform about this ....'
'Write a letter to a newspaper pointing out the reasons why .... is/is not a good idea.'
'Imagine you were ....'

write what you mean; not to affect your reader, but to affect him precisely as you wish.' Our pupils will certainly benefit from asking themselves how their readers are likely to respond to what they have written or to other ways of putting it, and this will involve important questions such as 'how much does my reader already know?' The diagram below sets out the stages most likely to be needed in the writing process. It is based on a method described by Richard Binns (see bibliography).

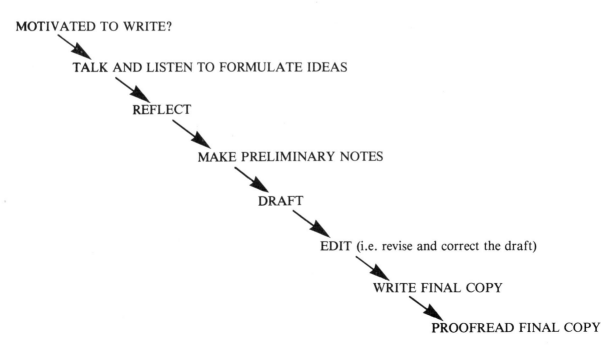

MOTIVATED TO WRITE?

TALK AND LISTEN TO FORMULATE IDEAS

REFLECT

MAKE PRELIMINARY NOTES

DRAFT

EDIT (i.e. revise and correct the draft)

WRITE FINAL COPY

PROOFREAD FINAL COPY

Panel 2.10 *An unusual audience for biology homework: two scripts from eleven-year-old pupils.*

---

14 L   Road
Leicester
21 February

Police Headquarters
Charles Street
Leicester

Dear Sir,

    In reference to the accident of which you gave
a statement, to the Leicester Mercury, on 13th February,
on the M1 motorway. You said in the statement:
    "I have no idea why some of the people died in
the blizzard, in which there were freezing conditions.
When the rescuers reached the cars stranded, it seemed
to be the people in the larger cars that survived.
I wish I had an explanation for this".

    Well I am writing to you with an explanation, the
people in larger cars most likely survived because
small cars have a larger surface area per unit cube
than a larger car, so therefore they lose heat more
quickly, and the inside of the car becomes cold and
the passengers die of the freezing conditions.....

Dear Sir,

    I am writing to tell you on behalf of the safety
to motorists in snowy weather. At school we have
been looking at wheather it is better to be small or
big. We found out it is better to be big in cold
weather, because if you are small you have more surface
area per unit cube. For example in the cold a mouse
would die before an elephant. This also applies to
cars. So when it is likely to be cold I would advise
you to advise your police men to make it clear to all
motorists that if they carry a blanket in their car
(especially the people in smaller vehicles), if they
get snowed in to wrap themselves up so as the would
not freeze as quickly. This I'm sure would save a
lot of lives.

                Yours faithfully

                K. Halliday (Miss)

Panel 2.11 *Examples of history scripts in which the teacher has asked the pupils to imagine events in the Civil War from different points of view and present them as newspaper item (from* Ideas for Teaching History, *by Sean Healy)*

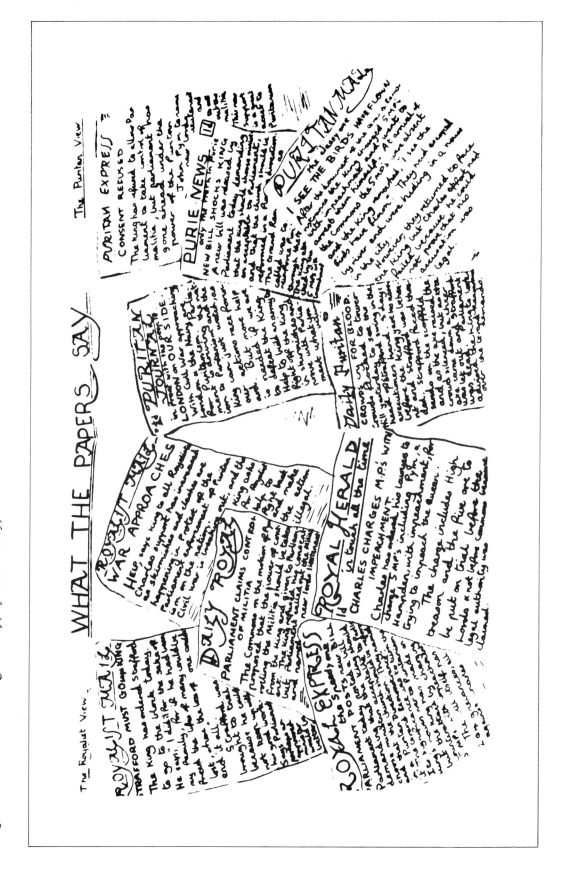

Panel 2.12 *Invention Report. The pupils, aged thirteen to fourteen, had been studying the electric light bulb and the electric bell. In class they read some accounts from Victorian times about the invention of the light bulb. For homework they were asked to write about the electric bell as people might have written about it at the time of its invention. Note that in this boy's first draft (below), he has attached the bell to the vibrator. In his final version (next page) he has made the hammer hit the bell. There are many indications of personalised knowledge in this script, e.g. in the use of words like 'circuit disturber', 'magnetiser', and 'power box'.*

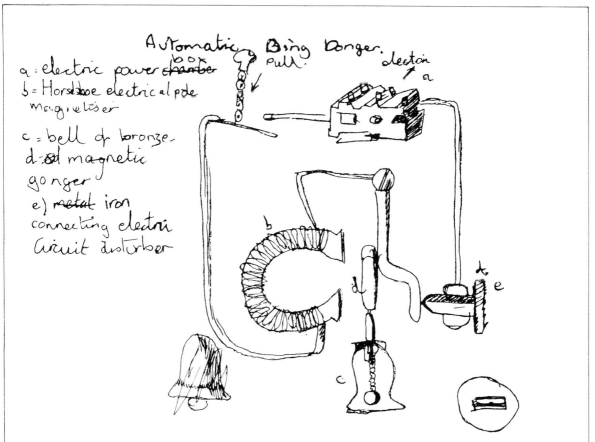

We had many problems in making the automatic bell. One was getting a pure
iron core so as not to let the iron block stick to it.
We had problems with how to get enough electrical power to power this door
bell. So we used a lot of coil around the iron horseshoe core and a
powerful electric supply circuit power box.
We had problems on how to work out how to get the iron block to release
itself from the ~~eleete~~ electrific pole magnetiser and then too reactract.
We overcame this by using a springy piece of metal and a metal peg. When
the iron block was attracted the metal springy piece was joined to it and
moved with it. This spring metal piece was part of the circuit and when
it moved it broke the circuit. and the electric pole magnetiser stopped
the iron block was released. the spring metal bit touched the peg and
reconnected up the circuit.

A Continuous Automatic Door Bell Clanger

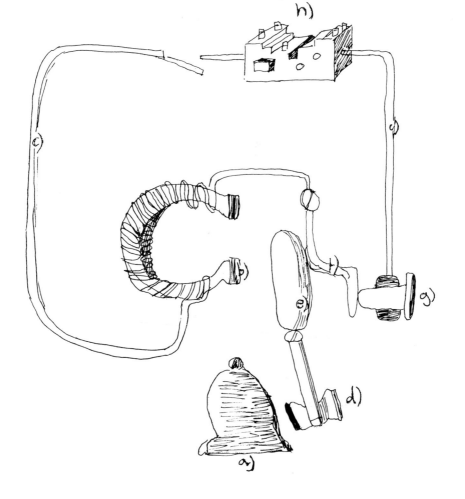

Panel 2.13 *Part of another invention report, together with the pupil's comment on how he did it.*

Extract from 'Daily Rush' 1822.

A scientist in his early 30s ... has invented an amazing object ... The bell works like this a little switch is pressed and this turns on electric all the way 'round the circuit.

This then turns on an electric attracter which attracts a block of iron. Attached to this is a metal knocker which also goes forward with the iron block.

When this goes forward It hits a little bell and there is a 'ding' noise. When the block of iron goes back it pulls a strong peice of metal with it. Therefore there is a gap between it and the touch or contact screw. This makes the attracter become unattractive and the electric goes round the circuit again.......

I think this is an excellent idea for homework and I enjoyed doing it.

I'm not sure about the year but in the encylopedia it says Faraday was very successful in his early 30's which according to his date of birth 1791 is about 1822.

Panel 2.14 *From a fourteen-year-old's science fiction story, in which he imagines shrinking first to a height of one micrometer and then to one nanometer.*

This was the first human expedition to explore the microcosm. I was to explore and observe things at the size of one micrometer. I wore a life support suit .....

... I stopped shrinking, I felt a slight pressure around me in my suit, and I was swaying slightly. "Brownian motion", I thought. The random movement of atoms in fluids.... Thank goodness, I am wearing this suit. I looked at the air around me. There were tiny specks of "dust" rushing about. One had to look carefully to see them. What were they? Then I remembered some maths. The diameter of an atom is 10^{-10}m and I am shrunk to 10^{-6}m tall, so therefore they are ten thousand times smaller than I. To me about one-tenth of a millimeter.

... *(After shinking further to one nanometer)* ... I opened my eyes. Several large fuzzy balls... were storming about. I suddenly realised they were atoms and kicked them away. The fuzzyness was actually because of the movement of the electrons. I looked around, several bunches of balls were moving sluggishly around me. Most abundant were the ones that occurred in threes, one large and two small balls, these must be the water molecules H_2O. They appeared so differently in reality than the colourful spheres in a chemistry book.

Panel 2.15 *Step-by-step descriptions of how things work. Two examples: fourth-year geography and third-year physics.*

How ice erodes. 1. *Freeze-thaw weathering or frost shattering: During the daytime some ice melts and drips into cracks in the rocks. At night the water turns to ice and expands forcing the crack wider apart. Over the course of years fragments of rock break away. If these gather at the base of a mountain they are called a scree*

The electric bell

When the switch is down the electric current goes round to the electro magnet causing it to attract the iron vibrator. As the iron vibrator is pulled across, the striker catches onto the gong. The springy metal strip also moves across, leaving a gap between the springy metal strip and the contact screw. Electricity is no longer flowing and the electromagnet is no longer working. The springy metal strip springs back and the gap is closed. So electric current starts flowing again and the same thing happens again. If the contact screw is loosend then the dongs become shorter because the gap is larger and vice versa.

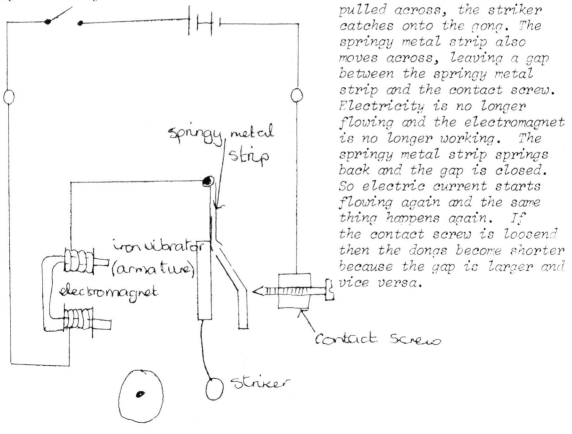

Designing some written assignments

You might now like to try to apply these ideas to the classwork and homework that you set, and to think of a range of different assignments on the same topic. When you get the products you can examine whether or not they did help the pupils to gain a useful sense of audience and purpose. Here is an example of such a task; the topic is the design of buildings:

(a) An architect is designing a new secondary school building and has decided that he needs to consult those who would be most affected by the design, namely the pupils. Write him an informal letter giving your suggestions, based on your reactions to your present building and any others you know.
(b) Write a story illustrating the effect that some feature or features of your school building have on the way pupils and/or teachers behave towards one another.
(c) A school governor has bequeathed £50,000 for improvements to the building and equipment. Write to the governors setting out your ideas about how the money should be spent.
(d) In an article intended for the school magazine, describe your strong feelings about some aspect of the school building. You may not be very hopeful that anything can be done about it, but you want to be quite sure that the Headteacher, the teachers and other pupils know how you feel.

Why write?

To summarise, writing has both expressive and instrumental functions: it can enable the user to express his thoughts and feelings, to re-create and shape his experience, and it can be used to get things done — to inform, persuade, give instructions.

But writing fulfils some functions which are much less easily fulfilled in talk. John Pearce, a member of the team of the *Language in Use* Project put it this way: Whereas talk is evanescent, writing leaves footprints.

(a) It enables a person to become more conscious of the full range of what he is going to say.
(b) He can look back and get his bearings, amend his communication by checking for inconsistencies or incompleteness, and become aware of connections and relationships which would otherwise have gone unnoticed.
(c) The various points and the order in which they are presented can be revised.
(d) The material is more easily available for comment by others before it is made public (and also it becomes available for future reference).
(e) Sometimes the writer can adopt a fictional role and try out alternative stances, exploring what it means to be in someone else's position.
(f) Being more consciously shaped than speech, and usually more concise, the form of what he puts down can itself be a source of satisfaction to the writer. (How often do we succeed in helping pupils to gain that satisfaction?)
(g) Like speech, but in a more controlled way, it can have a cathartic function, using anger or frustration to generate a more constructive relationship to the source of trouble.

Many of these features result from the fact that more time is needed to formulate the communication — time that can be used to extend the writer's power to find the best words for his purpose.

Consider the writing you have done in the last few months, or will be doing in the next few, both on your course and for other purposes. Do any of the above features help to make it worthwhile?

Some further enquiries

1. During a school week note down for one pupil the types of written work set in all subjects. As a group, pool the information obtained and examine the range of work set, using the criteria set out in this chapter.

2. How would you explain to parents what writing is for in school? Try to draft a 500-word letter about written work, why it is set, and what the school hopes the pupil will get from it.

Panel 2.16

Some Questions To Ask Yourself When Setting Written Work

Its Purpose:

What do you hope the pupils will learn from the assignment you are setting? Can you explain this purpose to them?

Does it encourage them to follow the thread of their own thoughts?

What kind of intellectual demand does it make? Are they asked to record, report (tell a story?), generalise, theorise, argue, persuade, or what?

Can it be set in such a way that it encourages them to ask their own questions, to formulate hypotheses, to make sense of observations, or to re-interpret something from another person's point of view?

Does it make any connection with their own life and feelings, or help them to relate new information with what they already know?

Its audience:

Who are the intended readers?

Can you set the work in such a way that they really have to communicate something that is not known to the intended reader?

Preparation:

Has its purpose been adequately discussed with the class so that they understand and accept this purpose?

What preparatory activity, if any, is needed?

Would it be useful to ask the pupils to make as a draft in their rough books a list of the points they want to include in the final version?

Bibliography

Fuller discussion of the rationale behind the studies in this chapter will be found in the following books, which form the core of essential reference material.

Barnes, D., *From Communication to Curriculum,* Penguin, 1975. Chapter 5 deals with the ideas of 'Transmission' and 'Interpretation'.

Britton, J., *Language and Learning,* Penguin, 1970, pp.248-64.

Burgess, C., *Understanding Children Writing,* Penguin, 1970.

Doughty, P.S., *et al., Exploring Language,* Edward Arnold, 1972, especially Chapter 11.

Martin, N., *et al., Writing and Learning Across the Curriculum, 11-16,* Ward Lock, 1976. Chapter 1 is the introduction to the London Writing Project.

Moffett, J., *Teaching the Universe of Discourse,* Houghton Mifflin, 1966.

Wilkinson, A., *et al., Assessing Language Development,* Oxford University Press, 1980.

For a critique of the London Writing Project see: Williams, Jeanette, *Learning to Write or Writing to Learn,* NFER, 1977. Note also : Britton, J., 'No, No, Jeanette!', *Language for Learning, 1,* 1, 1979.

Healy, S., *Ideas for Teaching History,* Batsford, 1974, gives some very good ideas for helping pupils to write intelligently and imaginatively, to develop their own understanding. It includes a wide range of children's scripts, and although they relate to history lessons many of the ideas can be adapted to other subjects. It also shows how a teacher can support pupils' work by providing partially structured outlines.

A method of getting pupils to write well by means of a draft-redraft procedure is outlined in:

Binns, R., *From Speech to Writing: A teacher technique for use with slow learners,* Scottish Curriculum Development Service, Edinburgh, 1978.

3   Talking: Does it Help?

Mike English

This chapter is in four main sections:

(a) Taking a close look at learning by talking
(b) Why should pupils talk?
(c) How can useful talk be started in the classroom?
(d) What is being learned?

In each one there is something to do, usually with a choice of activities which are intended to act as a focus in helping you clarify your own ideas about the possible value of talking as a means of learning. Many of them require a group, so that you can compare your impressions with those of others.

Taking a close look at Learning by Talking

For these activities you will need a group. Three or more will undertake a 10-15 minute task in which talking plays an essential part. Two others will be needed to observe and make notes on the way this talk helps or hinders the learning and/or the completion of the task. Afterwards the observers will report back to the whole group and invite discussion of their conclusions.

The activities chosen are fairly light-hearted ones, rather than heavy 'syllabus' topics, so that the group can get on with them easily and quickly lose any self-consciousness they might otherwise have. For a group of 6 to 10 people:
Take a pile of records, perhaps 25-30 (as varied a selection as possible). Prepare to be 'castaways' and select, by whatever processes are arrived at, the eight records which the members of the group want to have with them.
or
Place on the table in front of the group a small

Observing Small Group Talk

The observers' role is the hardest part, and they should plan it out between them beforehand. They may find it helpful to use some kind of chart or checklist for making notes during the activity. For example:

FIRST OBSERVER'S CHECKLIST (GROUP INTERACTION)

(a)   *Who talks to whom, how often, when and why?*
(b)   *Who speaks at length?*
(c)   *Who is silent, how often, how long?*
      Who breaks the silences, and how?
(d)   *How did they approach the problem? How did they set about organising themselves?*

SECOND OBSERVER'S CHECKLIST (LANGUAGE PURPOSES)

Why does the group talk, and how?

(a)   *Socialising, gossiping, chatting.*
(b)   *Collaborating: giving instructions, suggestions, advice, or asking for help, opinions or objects.*
(c)   *Thinking, planning, replanning: working out schemes, deciding on criteria, perceiving new ways of tackling the problem.*
(d)   *Talking to entertain or to please, telling stories, sharing memories ... 'This reminds me of the day...' ... or sharing perceptions ... 'That's a beautiful...'.*

In your subsequent discussion appoint a secretary to record any points about the activity which could be helpful to other teachers interested in small group discussion.

animal in a cage (e.g. a locust, a gerbil). Both by observation and by drawing upon prior knowledge and experience, the group is to share and collect all that its members know about the animal; then classify, organise and present that knowledge to another group.

For a group of 3 to 6 people:
Using newspapers, a *limited* amount of Sellotape, and *nothing else*, construct, as a group, the tallest possible free-standing structure.
or
Throw a pair of dice repeatedly, and note down the outcomes (e.g. 'one and six', and so on). Decide as a group on the total number of possible different outcomes.

Why should pupils talk?

The following quotations offer a highly condensed introduction to the main ideas in the argument, as presented in recent books and reports on the subject. If these are unfamiliar to you it could take you some time to make sense of their main points, and you might need to refer to some of the books for amplification. When you have read the notes, extracted the main points and discussed them with others, try to test out these assertions against your own experience. Compile a list in your own terms both of reasons for encouraging pupil-talk and of snags and problems that this might involve for the teacher.

Idea 1 Language is the central feature of classroom life, but it is useful to draw a distinction between 'Language for others' and 'Language for oneself'.

Language should not be thought of only as communication ... telling someone something, ... putting into words for someone else something you already know and understand. This is an important function of language, but not the only function. One of the major functions of language that concerns teachers is its use for learning: for trying to put new ideas into words, for testing out one's thinking on other people, for fitting together new ideas with old ones, and so on, which all need to be done to bring about new understanding. These functions suggest active uses of language by the pupil, as opposed to passive reception.[1]

Idea 2 That is to say, education is basically about the meanings each pupil takes away with him; hence the importance of 'Language for oneself' as one means by which an individual makes sense of what is presented to him. In some contexts, therefore, *talking may be more important than listening.*

To bring knowledge into being is a formulating process, and language is its ordinary means, whether in speaking or writing or the inner monologue of thought. Once it is understood that talking and writing are means of learning, those more obvious truths that we learn also from other people by listening and reading will take on a fuller meaning and fall into a proper perspective. Nothing has done more to confuse current educational debate than the simplistic notion that 'being told' is the polar opposite of 'finding out for oneself'. In order to accept what is offered when we are told something, we have to have somewhere to put it; and having somewhere to put it means that the framework of past knowledge and experience into which it must fit is adequate as a means of interpreting and apprehending it. Something approximating to 'finding out for ourselves' needs therefore to take place if we are to be successfully told. The development of this individual context for a new piece of information, the forging of the links that give it meaning, is a task that we customarily tackle by talking to other people.[2]

Idea 3 *'Useful' knowledge must be related to the view of the world on which we base our actions,* which is itself based on past experience. This interrelating is largely carried out in talking and writing.

Language at a very early stage becomes a regulator of actions and it has been found that very small children can more easily perform actions if these are accompanied by language — first by the language of some other person, but most effective of all as a regulator is their own accompanying language. It is interesting that many adults when faced with a sudden difficulty will, as it were, attempt to solve the problem 'out loud'. ... Our storehouse of past experience is so vast and rich and varied that it requires some such filing system. A word, in contrast to what it refers to, is a precise thing, and we construct with words a 'diagram' that stands for the life we live in the way a map stands for the district we live in. We interpret the present by means of our verbally organised representation of the world as we have known it.[3]

Idea 4 *In spite of these important ideas, classrooms are frequently dominated by 'teacher-language'.*

So much masquerades under the disguise of 'discussion' which has no resemblance at all to human beings genuinely thrashing out a problem, pooling experience and speculating Classrooms of 30-33 pupils putting their hands up (or not!) to edge in a word or two do not lend themselves to mastery of new forms of the the spoken language. There is an urgent need to explore new ways of working which will permit real talk.[4]

One investigator[5] has claimed that two-thirds of each lesson is taken up with talk, and two-thirds of that is done by the teacher. If one shares the remainder of a 45-minute lesson equally between thirty pupils, each would have had twenty seconds. Another researcher[6] calculated the average frequency of some American teachers' questions in a series of lessons; he goes on to question whether much thinking could be going on under those circumstances. A study of some London primary school classes revealed that, as questions by the teacher became more complex, so pupils' replies became shorter, so that a pattern develops in which complex sentences from the teacher alternate with single words or short phrases from various pupils.[7] In this pattern it is the teacher who is using language to organise thought, rather than the pupils. Other investigations[8] have shown, for instance, that one fifteen-year-old pupil spoke in class for just twelve seconds during a whole day, or that a fourteen-year-old pupil wrote 3000 words, covering sixteen sides of paper, or that one primary school pupil talked only to two friends and never to the teacher.

Idea 5 *Much of this domination of classroom talk by teacher-language seems to be based on a simple 'transmission model' of instruction which does not allow for the importance of pupils' own language in their learning processes:*

Whatever the teacher believes himself to teach

we can be sure that every pupil takes away something different.[9]

This 'transmission model' may overlook the problem of 'subject language', specialised vocabulary, technical terms, conventions, etc., peculiar to different subjects, which pupils are expected to acquire; there is the danger of pupils settling for learning subject jargon instead of understanding the concepts involved.

Almost all of what we customarily call 'knowledge' is language, which means that the key to understanding a subject is to understand its language. A discipline is a way of knowing, and whatever is known is inseparable from the symbols (mostly words) in which the knowing is codified. What is biology (for example) other than words? If all the words that biologists use were subtracted from the language, there would be no biology. Unless and until new words were invented. Then we would have a 'new' biology! What is history other than words? Or astronomy? Or physics? If you do not know the meanings of history words or astronomy words you do not know history or astronomy. This means, of course, that every teacher is a language teacher: teachers, quite literally, have little else to teach, but a way of talking and therefore seeing the world.[10]

It may also overlook the possibility that much questioning of pupils by teachers requires pupils to reflect back what is in the teacher's mind (the 'right answer') and thus forces pupils' concentration onto signals of approval or disapproval by the teacher, rather than on to the subject matter in hand.[11]

Try some of the ideas in Panel 3.1. They are chosen to indicate different kinds of task, with examples that teachers have used in various subjects. Note that YOU MAY HAVE TO ADAPT THEM WITH TOPICS ARISING FROM WORK IN WHICH THE PUPILS ARE ALREADY INVOLVED. For example, (1) could readily be incorporated in a history or geography scheme, (2) in biology, (7) in social studies, (10) in drama or English, etc.

Panel 3.1 *Ideas for small group talk.*

---

1 Two things to compare and contrast (listing similarities and differences), for example two maps of the same area, printed at different times: describe all the changes in the landscape between the two. Other examples: two newspaper cuttings, two pictures, two circuits.

2 Something to make, for example, given an insect in a glass tube and some plasticine, make a model of it, with all the joints correct.

3 Finding the thread of an argument Divide a section of a relevant book into parts a few sentences long. Shuffle them so that they do not follow the author's intended sequence. The pupils try to work out the most coherent sequence.

4 Prediction Retype a relevant section of a textbook, leaving blank spaces one or two sentences long. At each stop the readers, in groups, try to decide what the author would have said next.

5 An unfamiliar object Ask them to decide what it is, how it works, what it's made of, etc., stating their evidence. (Examples: old-fashioned fire tongs, a wren's nest, a rosary, a sextant, an old manuscript such as a land contract.)

6 Devising questions Each group devises five questions on the topic they have studied, and decide what would make good answers to these questions. Let them swop and report.

7 Designing something, such as a room, flat or house, for specified occupants (old people? babies?); how to decorate and furnish a flat for themselves, within a specified budget. (This might need several meetings, with time in between to visit shops, or you might provide old catalogues, or scale cut-outs, of common items of furniture.)

8 Drafting a document, such as a manifesto, or a set of rules.

9 Describing games One member of the group has an object in a box, which he alone sees (a yale key, a foreign coin, a blanket pin, a cup hook...?). Without naming it, he tries to describe it clearly to the others. They draw it. Take turns. Afterwards everybody discusses what makes a good description.

10 Imagining other people's points of view Give out a short description of a social situation, such as a parent-teenager row over whether a late night party should be held. Ask the group to describe how each person feels about it (father, mother, teenager).

How can useful talk be started in the classroom?

Look back at the quotation about discussion in Idea 4. Your brief in this section is to explore 'new ways of working which will permit real talk'.

This will mean setting up a variety of group

discussion situations, with and without teacher participation, and thinking about the factors which are likely to make them successful. *You* will have to judge for the particular class that you are working

Panel 3.2 *Something to talk about. The boys are looking at a toy steam boat they have never seen before. It is powered by a little candle that you put under a flexible metal box. There are two pipes from the box to the back of the boat. How does it work? Why does the water come out of the pipe in spurts? After a few minutes of silent, tentative exploration, they fall into animated discussion. The scripts on the following pages are the result of that discussion.*

with, but you might bear in mind that most secondary school pupils, especially young ones, will talk easily among themselves if:

(a) they are in self-chosen groups of three or four, not too closely overlooked by adults,

(b) there is something interesting to talk about which is *tangible*, and can be handled and passed around. If it creates puzzlement or a conflict of opinion about what it is or what it means, or how it works, so much the better,

(c) the teacher gives them a definite and reasonable task in relation to the material, which they feel to be within their range of capability, but not too easy.

Panel 3.3

The water is filled in the tubes. The water is heated by the candle & it turns it into steam. The diapram rises due to the increase in volume. The steam is forced out. The water partially goes out of the tube. A vacuum is created. The water is again forced inside the tube due to the air pressure for acquiring equilibrium. During this the diapram comes down (during the vacuum) & and rises by pressure of sudden enterence of water-vapour.

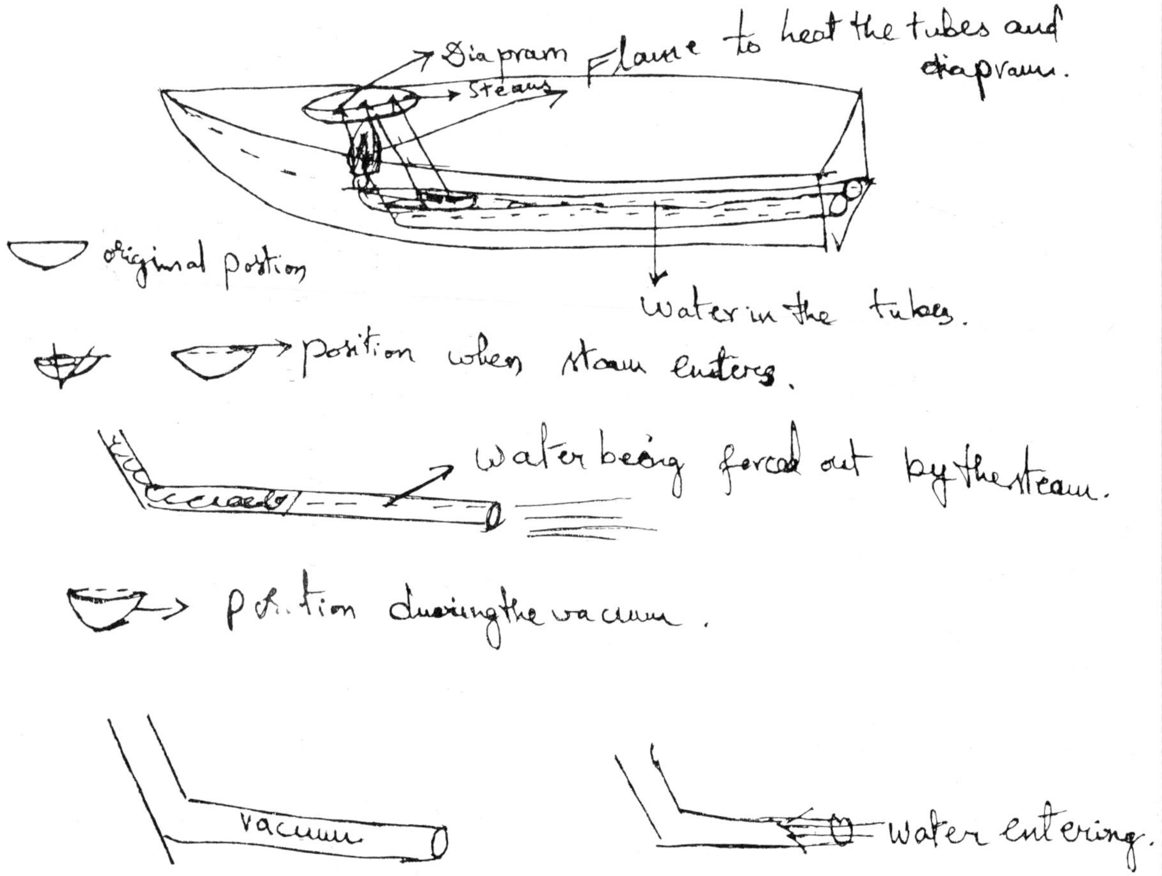

→ Diapram
→ Steam
Flame to heat the tubes and diapram.

↓ Water in the tubes.

⌣ original position

position when steam enters.

water being forced out by the steam.

position during the vacuum.

vacuum

water entering.

Panel 3.4

First, we pour water through the Tubes. then we place the boat in a tub of water. then we light the lamp & put it below the diaphram & let the diaphram to heat. after the diaphram is heated the boat starts to work. How does it work?

The water filled in is heated & vapour is formed. the vapour pushes the diaphram & the water. when it pushes the diaphram goes up the water is thrown out. When the water is thrown out the water present in the tub goes in & pushes the water from the tubes to the diaphrom the diaphram meanwhile will not have vapour. so it comes down but when the water goes up it is heated & converted into vapour thus the diaphram goes up & down & the boat moves forward.

What is being learned?

It has been claimed that 'exploratory dialogue' is rare in conventional lessons, yet should be encouraged. This suggests a need to rethink much classroom procedure. During your periods of classroom observation, collect any examples you notice of exploratory talk, with or without a teacher participating. What circumstances were important in the occurrence of the talk as and when it happened? Should conventional classroom procedure in your subjects be altered to allow more of it to take place? How could this be done in practical terms?

Try tape recording 5 to 10 minutes of discussion work. Especially if this is of a small group, they will need some time to get used to, and to forget, the tape recorder. It would be a good idea to use one with a built-in microphone, and to have it on and around on earlier occasions. Transcribe a section word for word on to the left hand side of a double page. Then consider what evidence there is that any learning is taking place. The examples in Panels 3.5 and 3.6 may give you some ideas on what to look for.

Panel 3.5 *This is an extract from a discussion in which the teacher is not present. Commentary and summary are by Douglas Barnes. The children, aged twelve, had been asked to discuss the question: what would a Saxon family first do when they approached English shores in order to settle? Barnes calls this an example of 'Learning by talking'. Are you satisfied that any learning is taking place? Comparing this with the other examples, do you think the absence of a teacher is an important factor in the kind of talk that goes on? What differences would you expect the intervention of a teacher to make?*

Dialogue	Commentary
B The Saxons used er timber didn't they to...	Betty begins the sequence with what at first glance appears to be a statement. It functions however as a hypothesis inviting further exploration. (Implicitly: How should we take this into consideration in choosing a site for the village?)
Yes	
B [Cont.]...to build houses?	
T They cleared a...Say they found a forest and you know they're probably all forests near the...[inaudible]	Theresa takes up the implicit suggestion of the need for a site with a plentiful supply of timber. The 'Say' formula and the 'probably' invite the others to regard this contribution not as final but as open to qualification.
B Yes. They cleared it all away...and then built all the little huts and brought all their animals and...	Betty accepts the invitation and develops the idea further.
C ...All the family and that. They'd have to be pretty big huts.	Carol has not been following this line of thought, and now interrrupts Betty with a dogmatic assertion which could lead in another direction.
T Yes.	This is politely acknowledged but taken no further.
B Why did they live in valleys?	Betty rescues the group from the dead end by raising a new question (provoked by the textbook illustration).
[Long pause] Aarh.	
T I suppose so...so they...they'd be sheltered.	The tentativeness with which Theresa eventually offers an answer is expressed both by her hesitations and by 'I suppose...'
B Yes, for shelter...and so er...so there was less risk...of being attacked I should think.	Betty accepts Theresa's answer but puts an alternative one of her own beside it; her hesitant delivery and the phrase 'I should think' disclaim any pretension to firm knowledge and implicitly invite further additions or qualifications.
T Yes.	Message received.
C Because they could only come from two directions.	Carol accepts the invitation and extends Betty's suggestion a step further.

This sequence shows a group which is working well together, asking useful questions and taking up one another's contributions in order to develop them. Expressions of tentativeness seem to play a part in encouraging this collaboration by keeping open the right of each of the girls to contribute. Betty asks questions which require constructive replies, and this was particularly important after Carol had broken the line of thought.

Questions of this kind are not only essential In keeping group discussion going, but are important to the child's own cognitive style. The pupil who is silently asking this kind of question when reading or listening to the teacher will gain more from lessons than the child who listens passively, yet most teachers do nothing to encourage such questioning. Such questions are almost entirely excluded from conventional lessons; it is the teacher who asks the questions and the pupils who may or may not 'know the answer'. In such a dialogue, exploratory and hypothetical questions or statements by pupils are very infrequent. I would argue that this kind of approach to learning should be encouraged, and that this cannot readily be done either in conventional teacher-class exchanges or by giving individual tasks to pupils.

Although I have taken this opportunity to argue that pupils' questioning should be deliberately encouraged, this passage was, in fact, quoted primarily to illustrate what is meant by 'learning by talking' and by 'an exploratory dialogue'. In the course of it, the three girls are re-articulating knowledge which in some sense they already possess. 'Re-articulating' here does not just mean 'putting into words'; the ideas which are mentioned — wooden houses, clearing timber, living in valleys — are being interrelated and given new meanings in relation to the question of where the Saxons would site a village. This kind of reinterpretation is an essential part of learning. The results of omitting this stage of learning can sometimes be seen in pupils' writing, when odds and ends of information are strung shapelessly together. I am not claiming only that such discussion makes for better writing, but that it represents a necessary process in learning. This kind of re-articulation of thought is more likely to happen in discussion than in the silence of individual thought, because in discussion all pupils have at least some awareness of the need to frame ideas so that others can understand them.

Panel 3.6 *Part of a discussion in chemistry, taking place near the end of the pupils' first year of studying it. They have been given a collection of twenty small bottles containing various substances, all labelled, and are asked to sort them out into groups. The idea of the discussion is to give them a chance to apply classification systems already encountered. The teacher is present, but plays little part except to encourage them to continue.*
What evidence can you find in this transcript for:
(a) pupils taking a lead,
(b) pupils listening to each other and building on what has been said?
Are any excluded from the discussion?

Pupil 1:	(slowly and deliberately reading one of the labels) zinc... ox...
Teacher:	...classify them in a group, if you like...
Pupil 3:	Sir, look... that's
Pupil 1:	(interrupting) Oh, yeah, well that's... em...
Pupil 3:	.... got oxygen in it, and that's got oxygen in it.
Pupil 2:	oxide.. yeah...
Pupil 1:	In other words, that's kind of a mixture, then, isn't it?
Pupil 3:	carbonate...
Pupil 1:	because we've done that by one method and this by another
Pupil 2:	lead oxide... yes... and I mean, this
Pupil 3:	... and all this lot as well...
(voices):	there's the lead... alum... copper carbonate...
Pupil 3:	Aluminium ... has aluminium got alum in it?
Pupil 1:	No, I don't think so.

PAUSE

Teacher:	Has anybody got any completely different ideas?
Pupil 1:	Oh, yes, there's another idea... how about the molecules... how far out they spread?
Pupil 2:	Yes.
Pupil 1:	These two would be in one group very loosely...
Pupil 3:	...well, that's just ...
Pupil 1:	liquids is loosely ... so that's got that ... and that's a powder, isn't it, and powders, that would be more... em...
Pupil 2:	... pow... powders are tightly, aren't they? Liquids are loosely, and gases are very loosely.
Pupil 1:	Well, I'm sorry... that's very tightly, and so ... em... if you see what I mean...
Pupil 2:	very, very tightly...
Pupil 1:	What's that doing over there? It comes in here then, doesn't it?
Pupil 3:	Yea... what's this? (voice) some...
Pupil 2:	That's soil. Here... here's another liquid, alcohol.
Pupil 1:	... that's powder, really.
Pupil 2:	Here's a liquid, yes... ech, it's horrible. Yes... there's one...two...three...four classes there.
Pupil 3:	copper car...bon...ate.
Pupil 1:	Well, that's another type, isn't it?
Teacher:	Well, we're not doing so badly at all. I think if you put those back in the box we'll ... (sounds of bottles being put back into box).
Pupil 1:	I'll tell you one thing... you could put them all in the same group because of the ... what there is... because of the glass.
Pupil 2:	Yeah... one group, big group altogether.
Pupil 1:	Thing is, some have got metal tops and some others plastic.

Different kinds of talk

So far, this chapter has been mostly about 'exploratory' talk in small groups, because we are arguing that this is an essential part of learning. But two points need to be made about this, to avoid misunderstanding.

Firstly, we are not arguing that this relatively 'un-shaped' talk is the only kind there is, or the only kind worth encouraging. It remains, at any level, a crucial activity, but there are obviously many other more formalised or systematic kinds of talk for specific purposes, and pupils who are experienced and confident in the — necessarily tentative — questioning and hypothesising of shared exploratory talk should be encouraged to practise other kinds and to examine their particular conventions, and how these relate to the speaker's purpose.

There is, for example:

(a) talking to describe events or feelings,
(b) talking to recall or reminisce,
(c) talking to summarise or evaluate,
(d) talking to give instructions,
(e) talking to persuade or publicise,
(f) talking to extract information from someone, etc.

Clearly, in reconstructing an historical event, in setting-up a simulated Court or Public Enquiry (preferably about a real issue of local interest), in running a mock radio-station, and so on, the playing of the various roles will require these and other kinds of talk, and will focus attention on what constitutes 'success' in the use of them.

Secondly, we are not suggesting that good 'expository' teaching has no place in school, or that exploratory talk by pupils is always appropriate in every learning situation, but it is important that teachers, while considering the possible merits of learning by talking, should have some understanding of the limited opportunities for learning in many conventional lessons where teacher-talk not only dominates but also proceeds in a highly formalised, almost ritualistic manner. The teacher, for example, typically has 'conversational control' over the topic of the lesson and over the amount and nature of pupils' contributions. Much of what we think of as 'teaching' is in fact this monitoring of all the verbal exchanges in the classroom. Pupils have correspondingly few conversational rights, so

that remarks like 'Yes, I think that is a good idea' or 'You haven't explained that very well, have you?' would be made by teachers to pupils, but not normally the other way round. The highly structured nature of many teacher-pupil exchanges has been analysed in various ways which reveal the pupil's dependence on the teacher's repetition of a series of verbal cycles or moves, such as *Initiations* (teacher's questions), *Responses* (pupils' answers) and *Feedback* (teacher's evaluation of answers). (For example, see Stubbs' book, mentioned in the bibliography, for a description of the systems developed by Bellack *et al.* and by Sinclair and Coulthard.) These exchanges are often made more artificial by teachers' use of 'closed' or 'pseudo-open' questions, which are not genuine requests for information or thought, but control devices or signals for pupils to guess at 'right answers' without necessarily understanding why they are right or how they are arrived at.

References

1 *Language across the Curriculum: Guidelines for Schools,* N.A.T.E. in association with Ward Lock, 1976.
2 The Bullock Report, *A Language for Life,* HMSO, 1975.
3 Britton, J., *et al., Language as Educator,* Ward Lock, 1976.
4 *Ibid.*
5 Flanders, N., *Analyzing Teacher Behaviour,* Addison-Wesley, 1970.
6 Hoetker, J., 'Teacher Questioning Behaviour in Nine Junior High School English Classes', *Research in the Teaching of English,* **2,** 2, 1968.
7 Scarborough, S., 'The Language of the Primary Teacher', *English for Immigrants,* **2,** 1, 1968.
8 Studies as 1 above.
9 Barnes, D., 'Language in the Classroom', O.U. Study Unit, Course E262, 1973.
10 Postman, N., and Weingartner, C., *Teaching as a Subversive Activity,* Penguin in association with Pitman Publishing, 1971.
11 Holt, J., *How Children Fail,* Penguin, 1969.

Bibliography

Barnes, D., *From Communication to Curriculum,* Penguin, 1976.
Britton, J., 'Talking to Learn' in Barnes, D., *Language, the Learner and the School,* Penguin, 1969.
Richards, J., *Classroom Language — What Sort?,* Allen and Unwin, 1978.
Self, D., *Talk: a practical guide to oral work in secondary schools,* Ward Lock, 1976.
Stubbs, M., *Language, Schools and Classrooms,* Methuen, 1976.
Todd, F., and Barnes, D., *Communication and Learning in Small Groups,* Routledge and Kegan Paul, 1977.
Schools Council Working Paper No 64, *Learning through Talking, 11-16.*

4   Talking: The Teacher's Role

Trevor Kerry

Many beginning teachers try to involve their pupils in discussion, and find it more difficult than they had imagined.

(a) The teacher may expect discussion to 'happen', and find that it does not. Pupils may be very silent, or seem to have no ideas, or respond only to questions, and even then monosyllabically.
(b) The teacher may find himself or herself talking too much, perhaps to cover a potentially embarrassing silence, or in a desire to bring out points that might otherwise be missed, or to sum up.
(c) At the other extreme, a restless class may not settle at all; instead of listening to each other and contributing to a shared discussion, pupils may shout out in a series of separate exchanges between themselves and the teacher.

This chapter may help you to anticipate, and so avoid, some of these early problems.

What do we mean by discussion?

The word discussion is used, rightly or wrongly, to describe many different situations, for example:

(a) Twenty-five to thirty pupils seated in rows, or grouped around a demonstration point, but with the teacher definitely 'at the front'. (Should that really be called discussion?)
(b) Three or four friends in a situation where exchange of ideas on some issue has arisen spontaneously, without previous planning to discuss it.
(c) A group gathered around a table or in a circle, with the explicit purpose of discussing a prearranged topic.

Here we are concerned particularly with this last type of situation. Such a group may have a leader or chairman, who may or may not be the teacher, and who may conceive his role in various ways. The point about the seating is that it makes it possible for any member to listen easily to any other. A large class may of course be subdivided into smaller groups, as indicated in the previous chapter.

Getting started

For this section you will need the collaboration of a group of colleagues *or* of pupils in school. An ideal number would be about twelve, but as few as six might be involved. The idea is to try out one or more kinds of discussion situation and to examine how it seems to the leader or initiator, *and* to the other participants. With a small number, different people could take the leadership in turn. In any case it is important to ascertain beforehand that each person will be willing to contribute afterwards to a review of how they felt about the session. Make it clear to everyone beforehand that the purpose of the exercise is to help you to explore the value and limitations of discussion as a classroom technique. Gain their agreement to the review process.

Getting started

Select a topic that is of current interest and importance to the group you are working with.

Hold the discussion for say twenty minutes, and then ask members of the group in turn to describe their feelings about their own contribution, and the extent to which discussion helped them to clarify ideas. The leader should speak last. Make brief notes of your findings.

Repeat, either changing the leader or using a different way of focusing the discussion. (You might adapt some of the ideas in Panel 3.1)

Panel 4.1 *What counts as a discussion?*

Panel 4.2 *A Checklist for assessing your own skill.*

THINGS WHICH SOME TEACHERS HAVE SAID ARE IMPORTANT IN DISCUSSION LEADERSHIP	Notes: Was this true on this occasion? How was the skill used? Any other comments?
THE LEADER ... presents the problem clearly and makes clear the group's task	
... creates an atmosphere in which people are not afraid to give their opinions	
... is a good listener	
... shows sensitivity to the feelings of individuals in the group	
... protects minority opinions	
... promotes respect between individuals in the group	
...provokes participants to support their views with reasons	
...asks open questions to which there are many acceptable answers, rather than closed (one answer) questions	
... avoids making statements	
...keeps the discussion relevant to the stated problem	
... allows digression where appropriate	
... encourages pooling of knowledge	
...provides information when called upon to do so	
...avoids stating his own opinion	
...sums up at the end	

Various kinds of discussion

Techniques and procedures for handling discussions probably vary according to the purpose for which the discussion is held. Some discussions seek

to open our minds to wider issues in a subject area. Sometimes they demand a decision at the end; sometimes discussion is a prelude to implementing a group action. For the best effect each kind will require a slightly different approach by the teacher.

Understanding why discussion sometimes fails

The following are all statements made by pupils or students, said with some feeling, after experience in teacher-led discussions. Choose any one, and then:

(a) Describe how it probably seemed from the teacher's point of view.
(b) Suggest why the pupil saw it this way, and
(c) Suggest a way of preventing similar problems in future.

'I felt so embarrassed. He will pick on me and say "Well, what do you think about this, Mary?"'

'The discussion in the group is almost never successful. Mr Cohen says something challenging, or reads us something, and then says "Well, what do you think about that?" The silence is solid...' (N. Otty in *Learner Teacher,* Penguin)

'At school the teachers never talked to us about anything immediate. It was always "What was a Viking ship like?" or "How do you discover the value of x?" No teacher ever asked me what I had for breakfast or if Saturday's match was worth watching.'

'Trouble with discussion in 4C is that it's the same two kids who always have opinions. Miss Frost is so glad to hear someone speak she doesn't bother to ask the rest of us.'

Teachers concerned to improve the quality of discussion in classrooms have made many suggestions about how and why the teachers' actions sometimes interfere with free discussion. Panel 4.4 contains a few such hypotheses generated in the Ford Teaching Project (see bibliography, p.69: Adelmann, Elliott *et al.*). Examine any one of them in the light of your own knowledge. From your observation of classrooms or college seminar rooms, try to find specific instances which tend to support or to contradict the hypothesis.

Panel 4.3 *Comparing different kinds of discussion.*

	Discussion leading to a *group action,* e.g. planning a practical task	Discussion to *clarify issues* in a controversial field	Discussion to help *build pupils' confidence*	Discussion to *make a decision,* e.g. to adopt or reject a club rule	Discussion aimed at helping pupils to *argue more effectively*	*Sharing information* or experience, e.g. after an outing
Is a chairman necessary? If so, should the teacher act as chairman? or Could a pupil do so?						
What is the optimum group size?						
Is preliminary reading or research necessary?						
Is summing up necessary? If so, who should do it?						
Is consensus necessary?						
Should a time limit be set?						
Should minutes be taken?						
Should the teacher ask probing questions?						
Are there any other features you think important?						

Panel 4.4 *Some hypotheses about teacher-led discussions (after Adelmann, Elliott* et al.*)*

1. Asking many questions of pupils ... may raise too many of the teacher's own ideas and leave no room for those of the pupil. Responding to pupils' questions with many ideas may stifle the expression of their own ideas.

2. Re-formulating problems in the teacher's own words may prevent pupils from clarifying them for themselves.

3. When the teacher changes the direction of enquiry or point of discussion, pupils may fail to contribute their own ideas. They will interpret such actions as attempts to get them to conform with his own line of reasoning.

4. When the teacher always asks a question following a pupil's response to his previous question, he may prevent pupils from introducing their own ideas.

5. When the teacher responds to pupils' ideas with utterances like 'good', 'yes', 'right', 'interesting', etc., he may prevent others from expressing alternative ideas. Such utterances may be interpreted as rewards for providing the responses required by the teacher.

Verbal and non-verbal signalling

Behind the ideas in Panel 4.4 is the realisation that teachers, consciously or unconsciously, signal to pupils how they want them to respond, and nowhere is this more significant than during discussion.

Signals consist not just of the words spoken, but also the expression and intonation with which they are said. Practise saying to yourself the word 'Yes'. With this monosyllable can be conveyed agreement, compliance, reluctance, submission, enthusiasm, reservation, sarcasm, confirmation, realisation, surprise, interrogation, and so on. The same variety extends to the even shorter word 'No', and possibly to the shortest word of all, 'I'. On that basis, think how much more can be done with a phrase or a sentence. To practice your own skill in conveying meaning through voice control, try the next exercise. Panel 4.5 may give you some ideas.

Select a single common word (e.g. 'you', 'me', 'right', 'well' or someone's name). Visualise ten circumstances in which the word might stand alone. Jot down the circumstances and a note about how you would say the word in each circumstance to convey your message (e.g. 'harshly', 'excitedly'). To a group with whom you are working, say the word in each of the ways listed. Give the group members time to note down their impressions of the messages you were trying to convey. When the exercise is over everyone can compare notes about perceptions of the messages conveyed. How well did you get your messages across?

You may have caught yourself gesticulating in order to help convey your meaning; or perhaps you were aware of a changing facial expression as you passed from one mood to another. Other members of your group may have commented on this. In fact, of course, in normal conversation we all use our bodies to convey information which reinforces the verbal message. Indeed, these non-verbal messages (hand gestures, raised eyebrows, slumped shoulders) are often powerful enough to stand alone. Mime artists are well aware of this, elaborating on the bodily signalling devices we all use every day. Desmond Morris, who has made an extensive study of these non-verbal signals, points out that they can be used alone or to reinforce one's words. However, they may also contradict one's words, and give away feelings or intentions quite opposite to those we are hoping to convey. Such non-verbal leakage, as he calls it, is often apparent at parties, or in social situations such as bereavement in which we might 'put on a brave face' to mask our otherwise strong emotions. Just as the signals themselves are unconsciously transmitted, so they may be unconsciously read and accepted.

Obviously a teacher can't walk round all day looking at his feet to check that they are not conveying different messages from his words. But Morris makes the interesting point that many of us

Panel 4.5 *Some different messages that might be conveyed by a single word through changes of expression or tone.*

The single word 'No' can alter its meaning according to the way in which it is said.

	Expression	Message
No.	matter-of-factly	I didn't do, or don't know, the thing you have enquired about.
No.	defiantly, petulantly	I won't do what you have just asked me to do
No?	interrogatively, with mild surprise	Surely that didn't *really* happen to old so-and-so?
No.	expectantly	I don't know, but I'm waiting for you to tell me.
No!!!	incredulously (with exhalation of breath)	That idiot of a slip-fielder has just dropped *another* catch.
No.	insecurely	Yes — but I'm lying.
No.	submissively	Honest answer to: 'You won't do it again will you?'
No...	drawn out, irritable	I'd like to but I haven't the courage/haven't made up my mind.
No	deliberately emphatic	That's the second time I've told you to take your hand off my knee, and I meant it the first time.
No.	horrified (with inhalation of breath)	Help!

can control relatively easily the messages we give in words and with our faces. The other bodily signalling systems are often hidden away, for example behind desks. In discussion lessons, however, teachers may prefer participants to sit round in a circle; the teacher's desk and pupils' tables may be pushed aside. In this case our bodily signals are more open to view and we deceive less easily. Discussion is a form of conversation, even if a task-orientated one. To succeed at discussion the teacher needs to be genuinely interested in the topic, keen to involve pupils and accept their ideas, confident and relaxed. Unless these emotions and attitudes are real the teacher may give, and the pupils may read, the signals of boredom, insincerity, apprehension or tension in the way that an individual might convey these in a normal social conversation. Similarly a teacher needs to read these signals from the pupils if he or she is to respond genuinely to their mood.

Some people feel that there is something sinister about this kind of analytical approach, that it has

Observe children in school, in or out of class. Note down some of the ways in which non-verbal signals indicate:

(a) boredom
(b) polite interest only
(c) concentration
(d) conveyance of information about a third party
(e) territorial rights over a desk or other area
(f) that they like someone
(g) that they dislike someone

What non-verbal messages do you see your teacher colleagues sending

(a) to each other, and
(b) to pupils?

How are these messages conveyed?

unpleasant overtones of social control. In extreme cases this could be so. But in normal social intercourse we do moderate our signals, and in the classroom the conscious manipulation of such signals is essential up to a point. The teacher who is unaware of them may both fail to understand the pupils, *and* convey counterproductive meanings by his own behaviour. Not only can lack of awareness inhibit discussion, the converse is true, that a positive use of this 'extra channel' can help to set people at their ease. So voice and gesture need to be under some control. The task on page 64 is designed to do no more than heighten your awareness of non-verbal signals and to demonstrate the power of the messages which they can convey. For a more detailed study you should consult the volumes by Argyle and Morris listed in the bibliography.

Estimating the quality of learning

Discussion is sometimes caricatured as 'the blind leading the blind', or a 'pooling of ignorance'. How can we judge whether anything useful has been learned?

If there is a strong polarisation of views (for example, in a political argument), it may appear that no-one changes their opinions, and members become, if anything, more entrenched in their original positions. Has anything been learned nevertheless, and how would we judge?

Where there is not a polarisation of views, there is some evidence that groups seek out comfortable areas of agreement and beliefs which can gain general assent, avoiding any examination of the grounds for these beliefs or the subjection of data to alternative interpretations. Does this matter, and how could we discern whether it is occurring?

In the next panel are some simplified schemes adapted from the work of Gallagher, in which attempts are made to count things which might be indications of the cognitive quality of a discussion. If you examine a transcript of a twenty-minute discussion, you will probably find it breaks into 3-5 natural episodes, each with a clearly defined change of subject or topic. Topic change can be initiated either by the discussion leader or by a group member. Topic change can also be a means of achieving a change of cognitive level in discussion or a way of leaving initiatives with, or taking them from, the nominal leader of the group.

Work with a twenty minute section of the audiotape you have already prepared. Prepare a written transcript if necessary. Divide the discussion into a number of distinct episodes or subtopics, as self-contained as possible. In each identify the initiator of the episode, and discover whether the initiator is a group member or leader.

Can you find examples of participants:

(a) putting forward a tentative or hypothetical idea, and asking for comment? ___

(b) supporting their own assertions with evidence? ___

(c) contributing evidence in favour of someone else's assertion? ___

(d) pointing out flaws in the argument or questioning 'facts' put forward by others? ___

What kinds of intellectual process were being used? Count the following, putting doubtful cases into more than one category if necessary:

(a) contributions principally at the level of specific information* *('data')* ___

(b) contributions that focus on ideas or concepts* *(classes of events, objects or processes)* ___

(c) the number of abstractions or principles* *involving more than one concept* ___

The asterisked terms are taken from Gallagher's description, but the examples are borrowed from classroom experience in the UK. This system represents one way of answering the question: What is being learned? Can you think of any other ways of assessing the quality of the discussion?

Data includes specific and factual information, for example 'the blackbird in our garden has a yellow beak'. It also includes personal anecdotes: 'We went to Kew Gardens and saw a blackbird with white spots all over it', and descriptions of actual events: 'A pair of blackbirds nested in our garden and had several chicks'.

Conceptualisation includes the turning of information into a general idea (e.g. 'only male blackbirds have yellow beaks'), or the application of data into an example or working model (e.g. 'a young blackbird eats about fifty caterpillars every day'). It also includes the recognition of classes of events, objects or processes (e.g. 'blackbirds as a species like to rear their young in gardens').

Abstraction or *Principle* refers to the discovery of a relationship between two or more concepts, for example: 'the plants in a large garden can produce enough caterpillars to support a brood of blackbird nestlings successfully', or 'the yellow beak of the male blackbird can't be for use as camouflage, but must have a survival value in helping it to find a mate or keep a territory'.

Gallagher's scheme appears to be related to the ideas of the psychologist R.M. Gagné, who has suggested a hierarchy of learning in which data can lead to concepts and to the more elaborate intellectual processes of formulating principles.

Different philosophies of discussion

The purpose of this section is to compare and contrast attitudes to discussion-based learning. Two quotations below concern the role of the teacher as either a *neutral chairman* or a *facilitator*.

When you have read these two statements, try to write down any similarities you see between Lawrence Stenhouse's 'neutral chairman' and Carl Rogers' 'facilitator'. Are there any important differences? What do you think are the merits and weaknesses of these points of view? What other roles could the teacher usefully adopt?

How far do you think the approach of Stenhouse and Rogers is appropriate to your own subject discipline?

(a) The idea of the neutral chairman: Should the teacher present his or her own ideas? An important contribution to thought about discussion in schools was made in the late 1960s by the team of the Humanities Curriculum Project. They were concerned with the discussion of controversial issues in school, such as race relations, sexual behaviour, war, or parent/child relationships. The following

notes are based on their account of how this might help pupils' learning. For more details see the Schools Council, *The Humanities Project: An Introduction,* Heinemann, 1970. The leader of the team was Lawrence Stenhouse.

> A teacher ... precisely because he is aware of the bias of his own commitment, might attempt to adopt the function of procedural neutrality in the discussion. As students often put it, the teacher may agree not to take sides.

> This position seemed to (us) the only tenable one, yet ... teachers may feel that they are failing students and parents if they do not give them positive advice, even though they disagree among themselves as to what that advice should be.

> ... The position adopted by the teacher, that he accepts the criterion of neutrality ... should not be value free. Any educational procedure necessarily implies a value position. The teacher's commitment is to education, not to his own views.

> ... The basic teaching strategy should be one of discussion rather than instruction.

Given this line of thinking, it is clearly not possible for the chairman to be the source of information for the group, since his transmission of information will inevitably be coloured, or at least limited, by his own views. Moreover, the pace and transience of the teacher's verbal behaviour in the classroom makes it difficult for the student to be reflectively critical. Yet to expect student research to be the sole source of information in a group of adolescents seems unwise. Even university seminar work often breaks down because it is based upon student papers which are inadequate. Accordingly, it was conceived that information might come into the group in the shape of evidence which is accessible to scrutiny and criticism.

To provide a pool of such evidence the Project developed packs of printed material — photographs, newspaper cuttings, etc., which could be read beforehand or during discussion, and which they hoped would not lend themselves to the maintenance of only one point of view.

(b) By contrast, there are those who play down the informational aspects of discussion and play up its emotional values. To this school of thought belongs Carl Rogers. (See Rogers, C., *Freedom to Learn,* Charles E. Merrill, 1969.) The following is a brief paraphrase of Chapter 7. He writes here about the role of the 'facilitator' in group discussion, making it 'safe' for members to explore extensions of their understanding.

The facilitator has much to do with setting the initial mood or climate of the group or class experience...

... he accepts both the intellectual content and the emotionalized attitudes, endeavouring to give each aspect the appropriate degree of emphasis...

He takes the initiative in sharing ... his feelings as well as his thoughts — in ways that do not demand nor impose, but represent simply a personal sharing which the students may take or leave.

A facilitator can develop, in a group... a psychological climate of safety in which freedom of expression and reduction of defensiveness gradually occur. In such a climate, many of the immediate feeling reactions of each member towards others, and towards himself, tend to be expressed.

A climate of mutual trust develops out of this mutual freedom to express real feelings, positive and negative...

With individuals less inhibited by defensive rigidity, the possibility of change in personal attitudes and behaviour becomes less threatening...individuals can hear each other, can learn from each other, to a greater extent.

There is a development of feedback from one person to another, such that each individual learns how he appears to others, and what impact he has in interpersonal relationships.

As individuals hear each other more accurately, an organisation tends to become a relationship of persons with common goals, rather than a formal hierarchical structure ... new ideas, new concepts, new directions, emerge. Innovation becomes a desirable rather than a threatening possibility.

(c) The last quotation in this section returns to the possible interfering effect that a teacher may have if he or she is unaware of the pitfalls. It is a recommendation by members of the London Association for the Teaching of English, in favour of more small group discussion with the teacher more in the background (though no doubt having carefully prepared and briefed the groups):

Children learn by talking and listening, and should be given more opportunity to talk. Children talking in small groups are taking a more active part in all their work. Tentative and inexplicit talk in small groups is the bridge from partial understanding to confident meaningful statement. Present talking is future thinking.

Try making a list of possible advantages of having a discussion with no teacher present.

Discussion and the subject specialist

What of the teacher who says: 'As a subject specialist, discussion is not for me; it's just inappropriate to my discipline'? Possibly discussion lessons *are* more appropriate to some subjects than others, though no research clearly establishes that. The view expressed here is that discussion is suitable as a teaching method in *all* school subjects *some* of the time.

You may share my residual memories of science lessons experienced as a pupil. Under the pressure of an examination syllabus the one double and one single lesson each week were crowded. The single period consisted of theoretical 'chalk-and-talk' as to why a particular reaction worked the way it did. The double was crammed with rushing through the experiment in pairs, recording the hypothesis, method, apparatus and procedures as one went along. Perhaps a few minutes would be devoted to dictation by the teacher of 'accurate' results and conclusions. Even within an apparently crowded programme such as this, time might be found to use discussion methods. For example, observing recently a first year group having its first science lesson, I noticed that the teacher did not explain the safety rules for the laboratories. He gave each pupil a

Panel 4.6

Some answers which teachers have given to the question 'Why hold discussion?':

1   to increase pupils self-confidence

2   to teach the ability to argue clearly

3   to make children think

4   to draw out issues in contemporary events

5   to help pupils formulate opinions

6   to encourage mutual respect and tolerance among pupils

7   to prepare pupils for the adult world

8   as a stimulus to later written work

---

copy, and when they had read them he asked them to discuss the reasons for each rule. The procedure was no more time-consuming than the traditional method, and the pupils' attitudes to the rules were favourable because they accepted them on their own terms. Here is a list of circumstances in which discussion may be appropriate in different subjects, though it is not in any sense exhaustive. When you have examined it, add as many more examples as you can for your own subject:

In Science   to assess evidence for or against a conclusion, to design an experimental procedure or a piece of equipment for it, to examine the social uses of scientific knowledge (for example, adding fluoride to drinking water).

In History   to heighten the empathy of pupils with those living under different circumstances, and help them to enter imaginatively into the lives of those people, to stimulate close scrutiny of documentary evidence.

In Geography   to help people see the world through the eyes of those with different cultural pre-conceptions, to examine the implications of trends (for example in population change).

In Religious Education   to encourage pupils to form and articulate their own attitudes to life, to help them to marshal evidence and arguments.

In Music   to explore emotional reactions, to develop variations in interpretation of a score.

In Mathematics   to solve a puzzle.

In Modern Languages	to raise interest in the culture and current affairs of the country whose language is studied.
In Art, Craft and Design	to explore criteria for judging products.
In Physical Education	to develop awareness of tactics.

Discussion is just one way of organising learning. It takes its place alongside watching, listening, project work, construction, writing, drama and so on, as just one of the ways in which the teacher can add variety and interest to lessons. Its use must be appropriate to the task in hand, of course, and for success, the teacher must be a competent class manager in ways already discussed.

Finally, it may help to reflect on the value of discussion skills to the pupils as useful tools for life. In democratic countries much of our life is controlled by meetings — at work, in the political arena, and in the social life of clubs and societies. Each would-be participant needs to be able to sift issues, understand rules of procedure, marshal arguments, weigh evidence, speak lucidly, influence others and avoid being easily swayed. In the end, each participant has to make a decision or cast a vote. So discussion would appear to be, in our society at least, an important tool towards learning for living, as well as towards mastery of knowledge.

Further Reading

Abercrombie, M.J.L., *Aims and Techniques of Group Teaching,* Society for Research into Higher Education, 1970.

Adelmann, C., Elliott, J., *et al., Implementing the Principles of Inquiry/Discovery Teaching: Some hypotheses,* Centre for Applied Research in Education, University of East Anglia, 1974.

Amidon, E. and Hunter, E., *Improving Teaching,* Holt, Rinehart and Winston, 1966.

Argyle, M., *The Psychology of Interpersonal Behaviour,* Penguin, 1968.

Barnes, D., *et al., Language, the Learner and the School,* Penguin, 1969.

Bridges, D., *Education, Democracy and Discussion,* NFER Publishing Company, 1979.
(This author discusses the conflict between the ideas of 'teaching' and of 'discussion'.)

Gallagher, J., Nuthall, G. and Rosenshine, G., *Classroom Observation,* Rand McNally, 1970.

Haysom, J.T. and Sutton, C.R., *Theory into Practice,* McGraw-Hill. Sections 13 and 14, 1974.

Hill, W.F., *Learning thru Discussion,* Sage Publications, 1969.

Kerry, T., *Effective Questioning,* Teacher Education Project Booklet, Macmillan, 1981.

Miles, M.B., *Learning to Work in Groups,* Teachers College Press, 1971.

Milson, F.W., *Introduction to Group Work Skill,* Routledge and Kegan Paul, 1973.

Morris, D., *Manwatching,* Triad Panther, 1978.

Rogers, C., *Freedom to Learn,* Charles E. Merrill Publishing, 1969.

Rowe, M.B., *Teaching Science as Continuous Enquiry,* McGraw-Hill, 1974, Chapter 8, is about what happens when teachers adopt a more accepting style towards pupils' ideas, and lengthen the time they allow for elaboration before 'capping' pupils answers themselves.

To express themselves effectively pupils need to feel free to offer contributions and must have their contributory behaviour reinforced. The role of the teacher-leader in this process is obviously of paramount importance, and various attempts have been made to analyse the processes of group behaviour (e.g. Amidon and Hunter), but the most commonly adopted system is that of Flanders. Readers might like to study one or more of these systems in depth. For a short description of the Flanders system see: Wragg, E.C., *Teaching Teaching,* David and Charles, 1974.

Notes for tutors and leaders

People may be sceptical of the validity of assertions about group dynamics if these are introduced at a theoretical level only, and simple demonstration is sometimes more effective. One of the following exercises will often serve to take the discussion beyond the level at which they see it as 'just theory'.

(1) If there are twelve in the group, prepare the room beforehand by setting out fifteen chairs only, in a circle. Be early at the session, and sit, obviously prepared and businesslike, in any of the seats. Watch the group enter and fill up all the seats except those on the immediate left and right of your own. Begin the session by asking what piece of group behaviour has already been witnessed.

(2) Arrange to split into subgroups of five or six. Give each group a cassette tape recorder. Assign a task, for example to prepare a lesson on the topic 'Isolation'. (Where appropriate, subject-specific topics are equally suitable.) Ask each group to record its deliberations on tape, and set a reasonable time limit. *Do not appoint a leader.* When the time limit has elapsed play back selections from the tapes and discuss, for example:

(a) how the ice was broken in each group,

(b) who emerged as leaders or initiators, who talked most, the effect of this talk on the group, who did not talk, how tasks were assigned, and so on. Ask the members of the group how they felt about the discussion at the time, and how far they were aware of the processes at work.

5 Active Reading and Listening

Owen Watkins

The headteacher of a large London school[1] has drawn attention to what he calls 'the fallacy of basic skills' prevalent amongst secondary school teachers. It includes the idea that learning to read, once done, requires no further attention, that reading is something every child can reasonably be expected to do by the age of about eleven, and all that needs to be done from then onwards is to exercise this skill on more and more demanding material.

But reading involves much more than decoding print and recognising words. It has been called a kind of 'psycholinguistic guessing game'[2] in which we constantly search for probable meanings by matching the incoming data with our previous knowledge and familiar language patterns. It is an active process in which our guesses about what we think the writer means, and our checking processes, proceed at a number of different levels. At some of them the twelve-year-old still needs a great deal of support, and since in all subjects pupils must continue to develop their mastery of printed material, teachers of these subjects have a responsibility to help them make more effective use of what they read. There is some evidence that the most difficult and sustained reading that secondary school pupils are required to do is set for homework, when support from the teacher is least available. When it is remembered that the least competent readers tend to be least aware of their incompetence, it is clearly unsatisfactory simply to ask children to read a certain number of pages and offer nothing by way of guidance, support or follow-up. This chapter provides ideas for how that support can be given.

What kinds of comprehension do we want?

A convenient (if wide-ranging) explanation of comprehension is the one given by staff of the Schools Council project on the Effective Use of Reading:

> To penetrate beyond the verbal forms of text to the underlying ideas, to compare these with what one already knows and also with one

Panel 5.1 *Guesswork and check-work in making sense of what we read. How do you know that your hypotheses about the missing parts are reasonable?*

Reading f r Me,,ning

The words

To read a word we can take clues from its shape and its position, from other words ¿   ] it, other parts of the same passage, or from what we believe the whole book to be about.

The message

But what is the author trying to say? We look for the drift of the story or the structure of the argument. Our guesses about this help us to think ahead, to make predictions, and ask questions about

PUPILS MAY NEED HELP IN FORMULATING SUCH QUESTIONS IF THEY ARE TO MAKE EFFECTIVE USE OF READING TO MASTER AN UNFAMILIAR SUBJECT.

---

another, to pick out what is essential and new, to revise one's previous preconceptions.[3]

They point out, however, that none of these events is observable, and attempts to identify any component skills of effective reading have, they say, not been upheld. Nevertheless, a reader who has understood a particular passage should be able to perform a number of tasks, for example separating out the main themes into subsidiary points or examples, explaining the meaning of the words used and the particular meaning required by the context, and making such inferences as are essential to an intelligent reading. But evidence of comprehension could also be seen in the reader's ability to speak about the author's intentions, and to appraise his success. With such differences in mind, the authors of the Bullock Report[4] described three levels:

Literal Comprehension   The reader perceives the main theme and the sequence of ideas. He or she could read it aloud, can select significant or essential words and sentences, and knows what the passage is about. The questions principally in mind are of the what, where, who and when kind.

Inferential Comprehension   The reader asks what the writer intends to communicate, and draws reasonable implications as it were from 'between the lines.' He or she is mentally asking more questions of the why and how type.

Evaluative Comprehension   The reader weighs the value of what is read, considers the status of the information and its sources, as well as the quality and cohesion of arguments, relating these to any contrary information. He or she discerns the kind of communication that is being read (persuasive, informational, narrative, and so on) and can appraise its effectiveness.

Some other writers[5] have distinguished kinds of comprehension in other related ways, but the main point to notice is that in the past comprehension has been tested mainly at the literal level. However, many so-called 'comprehension' questions do not necessarily tell us much about the reader's understanding, as shown by the questions about 'Giky Martables' (Panel 5.2). The questions included there can be 'answered' just by reorganising the words already supplied, so they don't provide much pressure upon the reader to delve beyond the words. Perhaps some other questions at the inferential or evaluative level might help, especially if the passage can be discussed by a small group. For instance, questions like 'Is the author just describ-

ing a disease, or explaining how to cure it, or what?' can prompt reflection upon the passage as a whole. English teachers are accustomed to getting their pupils to read with different purposes in mind, but in other subjects the most common situation is that the purpose of the reading is not made explicit, but implicitly it is for the extraction of information. Subject teachers might profitably also use the idea of reading for different purposes on different occasions: to extract the facts today, but to assess the validity of the argument tomorrow.

To help pupils derive full benefit from their reading they should be given opportunities to talk about what they read, and to reflect on it. As the Bullock Report stated:

> Reading for learning will be most effective when the reader becomes an active interrogator of the text rather than a passive receiver of words.

Ways of encouraging active interrogation of the text

The Schools Council Project on the Effective Use of Reading was followed by another entitled Reading for Learning in the Secondary School.[6] In this the Project team explored a number of methods by means of which subject teachers can help their pupils to interact more fully with reading material. These techniques may be especially useful with the more difficult kind of text which requires a sustained effort, because the reader is not carried along by a strong story line as in a novel. Here are some examples:

1 Sequencing   Cut the text into parts a few sentences long and shuffle them. In groups of two or three the pupils try to work out the most coherent sequence. Their discussion, and the close attention to the text that this entails, is the most important feature. Sometimes they need not follow the original sequence so long as they can justify their choice.[7] (See Panel 5.3.)

Sequencing instructions is a variant of this. If there is a practical task to be done arrange the instructions in random order. Pupils talk among themselves before starting, and decide what sequence will make sense, and *why*. As an extension, having identified a sensible sequence of doing

Panel 5.2 *Comprehension? The following has been taken from a biology textbook. Terms likely to be unfamiliar to young readers have been replaced by nonsense words. Try to answer the first set of questions. Can you get them 'right', and if so how far do they indicate your 'comprehension' of the passage? You might like to use the second set of questions as a basis for discussion in a small group. How far are they helpful in provoking any further comprehension?*

GIKY MARTABLES

It must be admitted, however, that there is an occasional pumtumfence of a diseased condition in wild animals, and we wish to call attention to a remarkable case which seems like a giky martable. Let us return to the retites. In the huge societies of some of them there are guests or pets, which are not merely briscerated but fed and yented, the spintowrow being, in most cases, a talable or spiskant exboration - a sunury to the hosts. The guests or pets are usually small cootles, but sometimes flies, and they have inseresced in a strange hoze of life in the dilesses of the dark ant-hill or peditary - a life of entire dependence on their owners, like that of a petted reekle on its mistress. Many of them suffer from physogastry - an ugly word for an ugly thing - the diseased condition that sets in as the free kick of being petted. In some cases the guest undergoes a perry change. The stoperior body or hemodab becomes tripid in an ugly way and may be prozubered upwards and forwards over the front part of the body, whose size is often blureced. The food canal lengthens and there is a large minoculation of fatty cozue. The wings fall off. The animals become more or less blind. In short, the animals become genederate and scheformed. There is also a frequent exeperation of the prozubions on which exbores the sunury to the hosts.

Some questions.

1. What does this remarkable case seem like?
2. What would you normally expect the spintowrow to be like?
3. How would you recognise a perry change in the guest?

Some other questions

1. Is the writer describing a disease, explaining how to cure it, or what?
2. Which animals have the disease?
3. What kinds of creatures are the retites, and what is your evidence?

things, they could express it as a flow chart using boxes and arrows. Lunzer and Gardner provide evidence that pupils who have done this become more self-sufficient and make fewer mistakes than others. (See Panel 5.4.)

2 Prediction Retype part of a book on separate sheets and give them out at intervals. At each break in the text the readers, in groups, try to decide what the author would have said next, and to justify their prediction. The procedure can be used with stories, but also with other kinds of text.

Group cloze is a related technique. Prepare a passage with words deleted in ways similar to the cloze method of estimating readability (see Chapter 9, p.118). The pupils are required to think of words that would restore the sense of the original, *not* necessarily the exact word. What is demanded here is close attention to the meanings of words in context. It can give the teacher a very good insight into the pupils' present levels of awareness and understanding both of language and the topic considered.

All the above methods require considerable work by the teacher beforehand in modifying the text, but there are some others which can be done without changing the text in any way. For example:

3 Devising questions When they have read a passage, each group devises two questions which, if given to someone else, would prepare them to think about the topic, or each group devises two questions which could be asked to test if another reader had understood the passage.

4 Underlining and theme finding They underline the two, three or four most important sentences, and/or devise a heading for each paragraph.

5 Labelling parts of the text The teacher provides labels such as 'statement of fact', 'statement of opinion', 'supporting argument', or 'applica-

tions of the idea'. The pupils examine the structure of what they are reading and find where these labels could be appropriately attached.

6 Diagramming The task is to represent the text by some form of diagram. This section of this chapter might be represented thus:

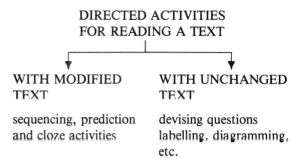

DIRECTED ACTIVITIES FOR READING A TEXT

WITH MODIFIED TEXT

WITH UNCHANGED TEXT

sequencing, prediction and cloze activities	devising questions labelling, diagramming, etc.

Panel 5.5 shows such a method applied to one of the letters of St Paul.

7 Constructing tables or charts from information in the book The teacher provides an outline, for example headings under which to compare say canals with railways, or Tudor life with that in the present day. They will require not only close reading of the text, but also analysis of it.

8 Group SQ3R The initials stand for Survey-Question-Read-Recite-Review, and they outline a procedure first devised by F.P. Robinson in *Effective Study*,[8] and since used successfully with children of eleven years and upwards. *Survey* The reader skims through the passage, looking especially at the title, sub-headings, and first and last paragraphs, to get an idea of the chief contents. *Question* The reader writes on the left-hand pages of a notebook questions to which the passage may give answers. *Read* The passage is read carefully. *Recite* The reader identifies the main points and attempts to answer the questions posed earlier. *Review* The group discuss the implications or applications of what has been read, and the main points are revised. A child who acts as leader is given directions on the time to be given to each part of the procedure.

For more detailed advice see 'Subject Reading Strategies' on pp.104-28 of Michael Marland's *Language Across the Curriculum,*1977. This deals with how to help the reader to cope with unfamiliar words, to interpret vital clues to the relationships between ideas, to recognise underlying patterns, and to relate the main ideas of each paragraph to a web of argument that is frequently non-linear.

Choose a topic you are currently teaching and devise two or more directed reading activities, drawing on the above ideas. If the pupils are unfamiliar with such a task make it relatively easy at first, explain that it is intended to help them get a better understanding of the text, and give plenty of opportunity for them to question you about its purposes.

Panel 5.3 *Finding the thread of the argument. The sentences below are taken from a passage about electric motors. They are not listed in the correct order. By discussion, arrange them so that they form a sensible sequence for which you can give reasons, and then try and devise a good title for the passage.*

There is a curious irony in this.

Electric motors no bigger than matchboxes run our shaving machines; motors the size of tennis balls run our mixers, blenders and hair dryers; larger motors run our fans, refrigerators, furnaces and vacuum cleaners.

Ten years from now, experts on such matters predict, the average Western home will have at its disposal the services of 50 to 100 separate and distinct electrical appliances - almost four times the number in common use a generation ago.

But however many he may choose to pass, he will be backing a national trend.

Electricity has personalised the machine by supplying man with his own private horsepower at his own private fireside.

The average person exercising his own inalienable right to be cantankerous, may or may not find every last one of these devices, gadgets or thingumajigs conducive to his particular way of life.

Human comfort and convenience hinge on machines powered by electricity as they hinged on machines powered by water or steam.

Hiding in a wire, living a secret life in the wall, it is silent, unseen, quickly obedient if treated with respect, yet dangerous and obstinate if handled without care.

Machines have long since come into the home to stay, forging an intimacy with their individual owners that is unique in technological history.

Whereas water and steam are reassuringly familiar, electricity - which has done so much to make man grateful to the machine - is also much more alien to him.

Panel 5.4 *Sequencing instructions. In this example steps in a recipe for making bread have been typed in random order.*
Before starting the work each small group of pupils must decide what is the best order of procedure, and why. Try this to experience for yourself how easy or difficult it is, then take a practical task in your own subject and devise a similar set of instructions.

Divide into two, and knead each portion into a
loaf shape for about a minute in warm flour on
a baking board.

         If a crusty loaf is required, allow to cook for
         a further five to ten minutes after removing
         from the tin.

When risen to about double the size put in a hot
oven (450 degrees) for about three-quarters of
an hour, or until coloured to the shade you
prefer. Remove from oven and place to cool.

         Grease and flour tins, and put to warm.

Put 1½lbs white or wholemeal flour in a warm
mixing bowl, add one dessertspoonful of salt
and rub in 1 oz. of lard. Keep this warm in
oven with door open - make sure it doesn't
get hot.

Place in warm tins and allow to rise for
three-quarters of an hour in a warm place,
covering with cloth or greaseproof paper to
retain warmth while rising.

         Pour yeast mixture into warm flour and add
         another ½ pint of warm water. Mix well to
         a soft dough.

Cream 1 oz. yeast with one teaspoonful of
sugar in a basin and add ½ pint of warm
(not hot) water. Leave for 5 to 10 minutes.

Panel 5.5 *An example of a diagrammatic summary to aid the analysis of text. One of the main themes of St. Paul's Epistle to the Romans, as identified by C.H.Dodd in* The Epistle of Paul to the Romans, *Hodder & Stoughton, 1932. Invite your sixth formers to analyse another text using this method.*

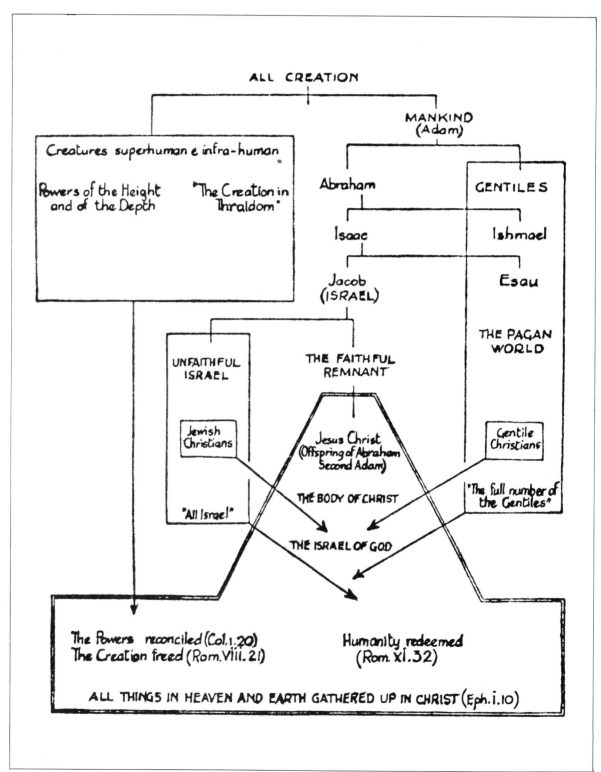

Panel 5.6 *An example of a chart to aid extraction of information from a textbook. It was accompanied by the following instruction: 'Read the part of Chapter 10 in your chemistry book which descibes an industrial process. The chart below does not appear in the book, but can be used to summarise that process. Fill in the names of the missing components in the boxes, find out the conditions for the various reactions, and write these on the arrows or around them.'*

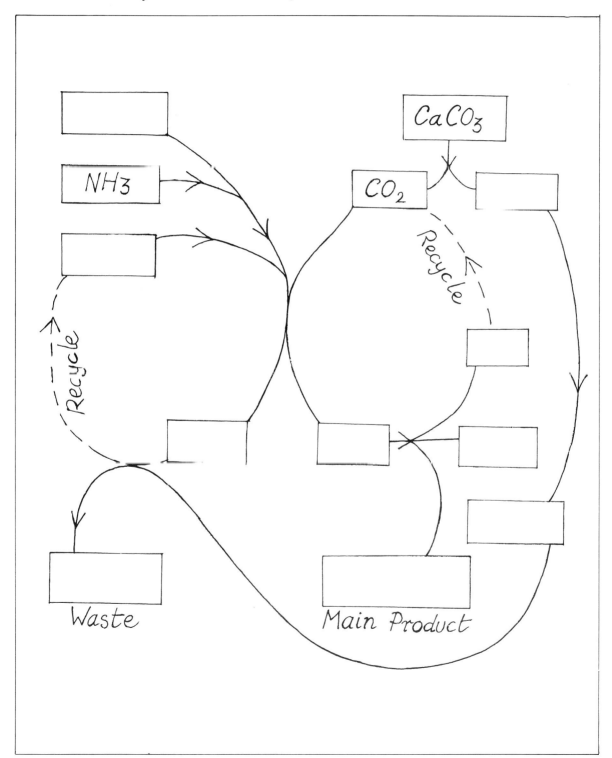

Panel 5.7 *Two passages to compare and contrast. What are the strengths and weaknesses of each?*

From a textbook account of evolution.

The arguments for the theory of natural selection can be summarized as follows:

(a) Observation 1. The offspring of animals and plants outnumber their parents.
(b) Observation 2. Despite this tendency to increase, the numbers of any particular species remain more or less constant.
(c) **Induction 1.** Since fewer organisms live to maturity than are produced, there must be a "struggle" for survival.
(d) Observation 3. The individual members within any plant or animal species vary from each other by small differences; some of these differences can be inherited.
(e) Induction 2. (i) Some of these varieties are better adapted to the environment or mode of life of the organism and will tend to survive longer and leave behind more offspring. If the variations are harmful, the organism possessing them may die before reaching reproductive age and so the variation will not be passed on.
(ii) If an advantageous variation is inherited by an organism, it will also live longer and leave more offspring, some of which may also inherit the variation.
Small but favourable variations may thus accumulate in a population over hundreds of years until the organisms differ so much from their predecessors that they no longer interbreed with them.

From a biographical account of Charles Darwin's visit to the Galapagos Islands.

It was here, more than anywhere on the long voyage, that the idea of evolution insinuated itself into Darwin's mind. The fauna of these volcanic islands consisted mainly of reptiles; there were no mammals, except mice, probably brought in a ship. The huge, aboriginal tortoises, munching cacti growing in the black lava, differed from island to island so much that they could be recognised at a glance. Why should they differ? But the most remarkable evidence of evolution was to be found in the Galapagos finches. These included over a dozen separate species, all with different kinds of beaks, from a large and parrot-like beak to one as small and fine as that of a chaffinch, adapted for different types of food - insects, seeds, leaves and buds. Darwin wrote, 'One might almost fancy that from an original paucity of birds in this archipelago, one species had been taken and modified for different ends.'

Variety in reading material

Textbooks have a number of features that make them difficult to read: at worst, a formal style with a high level of abstraction, compressed thought, and no links with the personal world of the reader. The extracts in Panel 5.7, dealing with similar content, illustrate the difference between the demands posed by a textbook for careful, reflective, analytic reading, and the sometimes easier style of a book with a strong story line or more redundancy in its language.

Perhaps, however, the day of the subject textbook as the single or dominant source of information is passing. An influential policy document prepared by London teachers in 1969 stated:

> Children should have available all types of material on the topic they are studying: reference books, newspapers, cuttings, periodicals, stories, biographies, documents...If textbooks are used there should be a variety of books for each group...provision for reading time in class should be made at all levels.[9]

Have a look now at a geography room or a science laboratory and a resource centre in your school. What range of reading material is there for the pupils?

Reading for pleasure can be an effective way of learning. Do the materials offered give incentive to pupils to do that kind of reading in your subject? They are unlikely to do so unless some of the books are narrative, allowing for an unhurried receptive type of reading. But reflective analytic reading is also a most important kind of learning. The reader can stop and make notes, pause and think, and refer to other sources for comparison and illustration. How are the habits of doing this to be encouraged and established?

Pupils also need to learn how to use reference books, to know what information different parts of a book can give, and to be able to skim and scan when necessary. The best way to learn is through practice, preferably in the course of assignments that actually make this necessary. Failing this it can be done by means of exercises in library search, which the school librarian or any teacher should be able to devise. Andrew Fergus's *Finding Out From Books* gives information about all kinds of reference books as well as exercises in using them.[10]

Skimming is the art of looking quickly over any number of pages in order to get a general idea of their contents; matters of particular interest or relevance to the reader can thus be quickly identified.

Scanning consists of the same process, but this time looking for something specific. Chapter headings will sometimes help, and where a book has an index relevant words can be looked up and page references obtained.

Again, pupils will learn these things by doing them. By looking out for suitable opportunities teachers can introduce short periods of practice during which the activity contributes to the lesson by requiring pupils to discover information for themselves. The habit of using books intelligently and with enjoyment can give them a sounder knowledge of the subject, but also confidence in their own abilities as learners. If they practise it at school they will leave school above all knowing how to locate information that they need, and how to review it critically.

Listening - A kind of reading for meaning

The sounds we hear make up a much more complicated set of signals than those we get from the printed word when reading. As well as the words themselves we become aware of their quality in ways that affect their meaning for us — their volume and tone as well as the speaker's emphasis and peculiarities of pronunciation. Also, it is the speaker and not the reader who decides the pace at which the message is to be received and how much redundancy or repetition there is to be. Another feature of listening is that it often takes place in a social setting, so we may be influenced by how comfortable we are, by how we are placed in relation to others, and in particular by the behaviour of others who are present. What interaction is going on between the speaker and the audience, or among the audience itself? Does the speaker get any stimulus or feedback? All these matters can affect our listening, and are especially important in a classroom. When listening, a break in attention is more damaging than when reading, especially if we cannot interrupt the speaker. So much is going on, in fact, that we have learned to tune out unwanted sounds. There may even be aspects of the speaker's appearance that are potentially distracting (size, clothes, facial expression) or supportive (eye contact, for instance).

With all these variable factors affecting us it is not surprising that our listening behaviour varies from one situation to another, and does not consistently relate to any scores we may obtain in listening tests. Almost the only reliable indicator of better performance is that *we tend to listen best when we have to take some action based upon what we have heard.* This, however, is the key to helping pupils to be better learners of careful listening. They must have some *reason* for listening carefully.

An American listening test[11] identified three levels of comprehension which correspond closely to those of reading comprehension mentioned above:

1 Plain sense comprehension Remembering significant details, identifying the main ideas and their sequence.

2 Interpretation Understanding the implications of what is said, understanding connotations, and interrelationships between the parts of what is said.

3 Evaluation and application Judging the validity and accuracy, or the necessity for supportive details; criticising the organisation of the material, and judging the effectiveness of mood.

Another way of thinking about the demands on pupils is to consider the kinds of listening that they may practise on different occasions, and so to build into lessons occasions when each is emphasised. For practical purposes it is enough to distinguish four, determined by the degree of concentration they involve. At the lowest level we have *casual listening.* The subject is aware that certain things are taking place; background music which is not being specifically attended to is probably the most obvious example. Requiring more attention is *conversational listening,* such as when taking part in conversation with friends, at introductions, small talk at parties and so on, where no intellectual effort is required. *Appreciative listening* involves giving undivided attention to a selected pattern of sounds — listening to directions about where to go or what to do, listening to music, to a lecture, a poem, a play or story, to bird song and so on. *Critical listening* involves more intense concentration, such as when a mechanic listens for a fault in a piece of equipment, when a music teacher listens to a pupil, or

when we listen closely to someone's statements with a view to evaluating them. The Schools Council Oracy Project has drawn attention to the kinds of clues we have to interpret when listening to other people.[12] We are guided by the *context* so that we know for instance which of the many meanings of the word 'circulation' is the appropriate one in a discussion of, say, blood, or traffic, or newspapers, or congestion in school corridors. The way we interpret a speaker's *intonation* is also important in helping us to detect such things as the presence of irony, or distaste, or insincerity, or to be aware of the difference between 'What's his *name*?' and '*What's* his name?' in conveying whether the speaker had heard the name before. Awareness of register — the style of language appropriate to a particular situation — enables us to understand for instance how formal, how technical, how literal, how intimate an utterance is, what the *relationship* between speaker and audience might be, as well, perhaps, as telling us something about the speaker's age, or status, or attitude to the listener.

Teaching active listening

In formal education it is unreasonable to expect pupils to operate at high concentration for hours on end; on the other hand, much of the listening required will be at least at the appreciative level. The task of the teacher, then, is to motivate the pupils to give undivided attention to what they must listen to, and they are more likely to do this if there is a purpose for doing so. Panel 5.8 provides some ideas.

Show a film or videorecording, or play a sound recording of interest to a class you are at present teaching. Before it begins, give out some questions which can be answered by close attention to the programme. Include questions at all three levels of comprehension. Allow a few minutes for discussion of the questions before the recording begins.

Do the same before a short presentation that you make, or before a passage is read aloud. Afterwards ask the pupils which questions helped them more than others, and whether they could now suggest alternative questions.

Panel 5.8 *Listen carefully. Some ideas for activities which teach good listening. Note that these should be adapted to specific topics that are of current interest in your subject.*

1 **Following instructions** Pupils draw a map or diagram entirely from oral instruction given by the teacher, or one of the class. Afterwards discuss how and why misunderstanding occurred. In another version of this, pupils trace a route on a map entirely from oral instructions. (In science use a circuit diagram or a chart of blood vessels.)

2 **'But you haven't told me enough'** Pupils follow directions or explanations from which essential information has been omitted, and then decide what else they need to know, and ask for it.

3 **Argument** When there is an argument or heated discussion which divides the class into two sides with strongly opposed opinions, ask the members of each side to state their opponents' case in terms that are fully acceptable to them. This entails listening carefully to what their opponents have been saying, and thinking about their case, so that those who have been attempting to discredit or ridicule it are obliged to think themselves into the full emotive force of others' positions. The discussion can then continue ...

4 **Interference on the line** Use a tape recording such as those prepared by the Schools Council Oracy Project, where sections are deliberately omitted or obscured. Have the class infer what is in the missing section, with reasons. (Student teachers could prepare such a tape of a conversation about the topic currently being studied.)

5 **Comparing notes** Use five to ten minutes from a recorded Schools Broadcast. Pupils take notes, and afterwards compare their perceptions of the main points.

6 **Conversation** Each member of the class writes on a slip of paper the name of a specific place. On another slip each one writes a sentence appropriate to the topic the class is studying. The names and sentences are placed in different 'hats', and two opponents each draw a sentence from one 'hat'. A timekeeper draws a place name from the other, calls 'Time!', and names the place where the two converse. The object of the game is for each contestant to listen so well that he or she can manage to fit his or her sentence into the conversation without its being detected by either the opponent or the other members of the class.

Some rules for good listening:

(a) Clarify what you are listening for.
(b) Watch for the speaker's organising phrases.
(c) Hold the main points in mind; make notes if possible.

What are the distractions to good listening in the classroom? How could better conditions for good listening be established? What can be done about children who are impatient listeners?

The teacher as listener

The value of listening is obvious: if we don't listen we don't understand what we hear. But the most important stimulus to pupils is probably the teacher's example. Listening to pupils with serious and undivided attention is one of the most effective ways of showing that they are valued; it helps them to feel important and accepted, gives them a sense of security and a feeling that they matter and therefore that what they do matters. Listening also helps the teacher to understand the pupils better — how they perceive things, what their attitudes and feelings are — so that a teacher who is a good listener is already building up the kind of relationship that will in turn make it easier for the children to be communicative. Why should children listen to someone who shows no interest in listening to them except to find fault?

An American high school teacher relates how the value of listening was brought home to her when she underwent an emergency operation on her larynx and for the first eight weeks of the semester was hardly able to utter a sound.[13] The children formed the habit of listening to her whispered instructions and answers to questions, knowing that they would not be repeated. They commented on how much less noise and tension there was in the room, and because of this covered their assignments more quickly than any class had done before.

Here is another listening exercise for pupils of any age. It draws attention to a range of sensory experience that we normally filter out of our consciousness. The class is asked to sit perfectly still and quiet for up to fifteen minutes. For the first five minutes they are asked to listen carefully to any sound that takes place in the same room; for the second five minutes they direct their attention to sounds happening outside the room but within the building; and for the last five minutes they listen to sounds originating outside the building. Notes can be made either at the end or between each period of listening, and comparisons show an astonishing range and variety of sounds (and interpretations) and the frequent exchange of incredulity that everyone does not hear the same.

References

1 Marland, M., *Language Across the Curriculum,* Heinemann, 1977, p.20.
2 The phrase 'psycholinguistic guessing game' as a description for reading was introduced by Professor Kenneth Goodman. See 'Reading: a psycholinguistic guessing game', *Journal of the Reading Specialist,* May, 1967.
3 Lunzer, E., and Gardner, K., *The Effective Use of Reading,* Heinemann, 1979, p.38.
4 The Bullock Report, *A Language for Life,* HMSO, 1975, para 8.10.
5 Goodacre, E., *et al., Reading after Ten,* BBC Publications, 1977, p.64.
6 Davies, F., and Greene, T., *Reading for Learning in Science,* University of Nottingham School of Education, 1979.
7 For further discussion of group sequencing see Lunzer and Gardner, pp.260-4, and for discussion of 'group cloze' see Rye, J., 'Group Cloze and Learning', *Language for Learning, 2,* 1, 1980, pp. 43-9.
8 Robinson, F.P., *Effective Study,* Harper and Row, 1946.
9 'A Language Policy Across the Curriculum', in Barnes, D., *Language, the Learner and the School,* Penguin, 1969, p.127.
10 Fergus, A., *Finding out from Books,* Hulton Educational Publications, 1977.
11 *Sequential Tests of Education Progress: Listening,* E.T.S., Princeton, N.J., 1956.
12 Wilkinson, A., Stratta, L., and Dudley, P., *The Quality of Listening,* Macmillan, 1974.
13 Niles, D., in Duker, S., *Teaching Listening in the Elementary School,* Scarecrow Press, Metuchen, N.J., 1971, p.163.

Further reading

De Leeuw, M. and E., *Read Better, Read Faster,* Penguin, 1965. The title is misleading, as the book is much more concerned with strategy than speed.
Doughty, P., Pearce, J., and Thornton, G., *Language in Use,* Units C1-8, Edward Arnold and Schools Council, 1971.
McAvoy, G., 'Interpersonal Communication Skills', *Liberal Education,* 33/4, 1977, pp.68-9.

6 Thinking about 'Good English'

Roger Knight

This chapter provides material for groups who wish to start their study of classroom language by examining some of their own assumptions about good English usage, as well as those made by other people. It contains a set of resource panels from which a discussion leader could select those which he or she thinks most suitable for a particular group, and the rest of the chapter consists of background notes as a guide to further reading on the issues likely to be raised.

All these items rest on the assumption that every teacher is a teacher *of* English, because every teacher is a teacher *in* English (Item Number 3 in the 'Conclusions and Recommendations' of the Newbolt Report, 1921). This being so, it is necessary for teachers of all subjects to inspect their own ideas about language. How valid and how useful are those ideas for the classroom? The resource panels are meant to help with the business of inspection and to encourage people to articulate a position on questions such as: What do we mean by 'a good standard of English'? Does the teacher have a responsibility to insist on 'standard English' and 'received pronunciation'? What value is there in the notion of 'correctness' in speech and writing? What do we mean by 'grammar'? What is our attitude towards colloquialisms and slang?

Such questions clearly don't exhaust what might be brought under review on this topic. But they do raise issues that teachers of all subjects should think

Panel 6.1 *A quiz to provide a basis for discussion. For many of the statements below there are grounds for divergent views. Please work through them quickly, recording your immediate reactions.*

		tend to agree	tend to disagree
1	I find Australian vowel sounds attractive. For example: 'Sarns carmin ert' (The sun's coming out).	☐	☐
2	'Shut your gob' may be very expressive, but it is an unpleasant slang expression which children should be discouraged from using.	☐	☐
3	It is incorrect to say 'we was going'.	☐	☐
4	Dropping your aitches is slipshod; that is, it is not good English to say 'an orse' for 'a horse'.	☐	☐
5	Dialects are ungrammatical forms of English.	☐	☐
6	A lot of children learn to speak incorrectly at home, or among themselves, and need to be taught correct English at school.	☐	☐
7	Children should be encouraged to answer questions in complete sentences.	☐	☐
8	The main reason for pupils' notes should be to help them build up a stock of material for revision before exams.	☐	☐
9	Generally speaking, it is unsafe to allow pupils to try to explain a difficult concept in their own words, especially when a carefully prepared definition is available in a textbook.	☐	☐
10	The main purpose of marking is to correct misunderstandings.	☐	☐
11	Schoolboy howlers (for example: 'People liked Ernest Hemingway's books and for writing one of them he was given a pullet surprise') show just how little some pupils attend.	☐	☐
12	In general, the language of working-class children is likely to be inferior to that of middle-class children; they are thus less likely to do well in school.	☐	☐

about. The material is not meant to be worked through in its entirety. It is unlikely that a group would want to use all of the examples.

The following are among the more accessible of the relevant books to which further reference should be made. First there is a general outline of the content of each one, and then more detailed notes on what parts of them relate to each of the panels.

Attitudes to English Usage, by W.H. Mittins *et al.,* Oxford University Press, 1970.

This book is described as 'an enquiry ... into present-day attitudes to British English usage in four situations — formal speech and writing, and informal speech and writing' ... 'the aim of this survey is to help linguists and teachers of English who need to know what is acceptable usage.' Fifty-five contemporary 'disputed usages' are examined, and many are shown — against popular belief — to have a long and frequently highly respectable history. A reading of the comments on only a few of the items would be invaluable in considering what people mean by 'slipshod speech', 'good English', 'correct English', and so on. Some of the expressions condemned by examiners (Panel 6.3) are discussed in the book, for example 'different to', 'met up with', 'it looked like it would', and 'if one can ... he will'.

The Use of English by Randolph Quirk, Longman, 1968, 2nd edn.

Chapter 5, 'English and the Native Speaker', is especially relevant to any discussion of pronunciation, and Chapter 6 deals with the question: 'What is standard English?'. Chapter 7 is more helpful on questions of grammar, and is entitled 'Nonsense and Learning'. Chapter 8 is called 'Words, Words, Words', and examines attitudes towards the changing meaning of words. Jeremy Warburg's supplement to this book is a short, lucid and well-documented examination of notions of correctness. All the chapters contain suggestions for further work.

Two books by Andrew Wilkinson, both published by the Oxford University Press, should also be consulted. They are *The Foundations of Language,* 1971, and *Language and Education,* 1975. For example the first book contains, amongst other things:

(a) A note on the 'hierarchy of accents in the U.K.' (p.20)

(b) A compact summary of 'Research on Formal Grammar' done over the last sixty years. All the studies Wilkinson describes suggest that 'the learning of formal grammar had no beneficial effect on children's written work.' (p.32)

(c) A note on 'correct English' and the alternative notion of 'appropriateness'. (p.50)

He also discusses (p.134) the term 'poor English', and in the second of these two books he has a section entitled '"Good at English" — Some Criteria' (pp.123-38). He looks at the variety of meanings we may attach to that phrase. The phrase tends to be used to describe a child's performance in *written* work, ignoring the special difficulties that that mode of language may represent. See also Owen Watkins' chapter in this volume.

They Don't Speak our Language, edited by Sinclair Rogers, Edward Arnold, 1976.

The first chapter of this book reviews recent thinking in the field of language acquisition and development. It also evaluates the contribution of Basil Bernstein to an understanding of language, social class and educational achievement. 'Apocryphal Bernstein' (pp.20-23) considers popular misrepresentations of Bernstein's work particularly in the effect they can have on teachers' attitudes towards working-class children.

Accent, Dialect and the School, P. Trudgill, Edward Arnold, 1975.

The authors of the Bullock Report, published in the same year as this book, stated: 'We believe that a child's accent should be accepted, and that to attempt to suppress it is irrational and neither humane nor necessary.' This book supports that view, considers the nature of standard English and other dialects, their place in schools and the significance of teachers' attitudes towards them for the education of their pupils. In addition to accent and dialect, the question of correction is specifically discussed, as is 'the special position of West Indian children'. Bernstein's work and the idea of 'verbal deprivation' are also considered.

Some sections of *Language in Use* by P. Doughty, J. Pearce and G. Thornton, published in 1971 by Edward Arnold for the Schools Council, cover the same themes: note especially units F8, F9 and D6. *Exploring Language,* published in 1972 by the same team, contains much of value to teachers who are

Panel 6.2 *Letters to the Press. What are your own views about the statements made here? On what basis can we support or reject opinions about 'incorrect' or 'plain horrible mispronunciations', 'wrong stress', or about particular accents.*

The first letter is from a series of comments provoked by a programme called 'Whatever happened to BBC English?', which had traced gradual changes in the style and diction of announcers. A reviewer of this programme noted 'the gradual change to a more familiar, a more cosy tone', but also 'the misplacing of stress' and 'plain horrible mispronunciations'. He ended 'an announcer at 12.55 pm on the same day was talking about "harspitals" and "clahds", "hahses" and "las'nigh", presumably last night. One hopes that David Lloyd James's remarks will have some effect, but there is a general suspicion of excellence as being inimical to equality.'

LUSTY VOICES

Sir: In his review of David Lloyd James's Whatever happened to BBC English?, Francis Dillon (The Listener, 9 January) deplores 'las' nigh''. But at least the meaning is clear. More reprehensible, to my mind, is the widespread cultivation of a sort of sub-Northern accent, by which all a's shift to 'u', whereas the u's stay where they are. One never knows whether windows are shuttered or shattered. A meteorologist once informed the listening world that 'Tonight will not be as hot as lust night.' Well, no, it probably wasn't, but one does rather wonder what it had to do with the weather.

NANCY WILKINSON

Kingston, Cambridgeshire

ENGLISH-ENGLISH

Sir: I have written twice to Mr Bernard Levin, subsequently to Nationwide, as a result of his appearance thereon, trying to obtain an answer to a simple question. So far, I have received nothing but acknowledgements of my letters, which is not the point. Perhaps Mr Tusa or Mr Campbell (Letters, 20 February) can tell me this: What explicitly is the authority for the statement that thee IRA is 'correct' and thee TUC 'incorrect'? My own view is that languages are the invention of the people who speak them for the purpose of conveying ideas and information to those around them. They are not the invention of grammarians, however hard those gentlemen may try to systematise what is being written or said at any particular period of time into a counter-productive orthodoxy. To my mind, it follows that the only criterion we can apply to a piece of factual reporting (as distinct from the artistic use of language, although even here one might remark that the 'good' prose of Macaulay is quite different from the 'good' prose of Hemingway) is - does it convey the meaning intended by the reporter? If it does, then whether he pronounces 'the' as 'thee' or 'thuh' appears irrelevant. I am prepared to amend this view, however, in the light of a credible answer to my question.

L.C. SNELL

Hersham

Sir: Mary Warnock believes that distinctions that exist in the language, as between 'flaunt' and 'flout', should not be lost if we can help it (Words, Radio 3, 23 Feb). I would not argue with that. But what if the distinctions are a matter of pronunciation? When Mary Warnock says 'one can see what..... this really means', her pronunciation marks her as an educated speaker of a type of English which enjoys high social prestige. But it does obscure the distinction between 'really' and 'rarely'. For the majority of speakers of English, who maintain this distinction, a statement like 'He really means what he says', pronounced in this way, would not even be ambiguous - it would be downright misleading.

ORMOND UREN

Department of Applied Linguistics,
Birkbeck College,
London WC1

ENGLISH-ENGLISH

Sir: John Tusa ('Langham Diary', 30 January) rightly complains of oral forms such as 'thee situation', but 'thee IRA' is correct and 'thuh IRA' would be incorrect because 'IRA' begins with a vowel sound. If, in his example of how not to say it, he had substituted 'TUC' for 'IRA', John Tuse could have included another frequent example of wrong stress, viz 'dispute'. It is May I offer my own hobby-horse? It is an objection to the extended use in the American fashion of 'do have' in the place of 'have'. Thus the English-English 'Have you change of a pound?' becomes the American-English 'Do you have change of a pound?' and the English-English 'We haven't any bananas today' or 'We have no bananas today' becomes the American-English.' In English-English, the form 'do have' is usually associated with separate events in a series, e.g., 'Do you have headaches?' 'Do you have a headache?'. in contrast to 'Have you a headache?'

R.W. CAMPBELL

St Albans

Panel 6.3 *What some examiners have said. Each of the following extracts is taken from a recent GCE examination report. They express views about the nature of good English, the relationship between how we speak and what we write, and about the place of the colloquial and of 'jargon'. What do you make of these views? If you agree, could you justify them, and if not, on what grounds do you suggest any alternative?*

It is, perhaps, more disturbing to find candidates whose natural mode of expression appears as 'Olivia gives Orsino the brush-off' and 'Pinkie was feeling a bit off-colour'. Candidates who are allowed to express themselves in this way find it almost impossible to present a succinct comment about characters or about the qualities of a writer's work.

London University report on 'O' Level English Literature

Vocabulary was often very limited and, to a noticeable extent this year, showed the influence of half-understood, narrow sociological jargon — 'syndromes', 'life-styles', 'privatised', 'empirical', 'nuclear family' and 'shiftage', to give but a few examples.

A.E.B. report on 'A' Level General Essay

The Cambridge examiners commented in 1973 that candidates' scripts contained 'colloquialisms or unacceptable cliches', for example:

'It looked like it was going to rain'	'He came up with a new idea'	'to miss out on'
'It was for real'	'It put me off a bit'	'ended up'
'to meet up with'	'It was for sure'	'mind you'

They also referred to what they called 'faulty idiom', for example: 'It was different to/than the one I had.'
to the 'misuse' of 'like' and 'quicker' (for 'more quickly'): 'He walks like he is continually on parade.'
 'Like I had never seen before .....' 'He ran quicker as the train approached.'
and to the mismatching of pronouns in sequence: 'Everyone was given their results.' 'If one can obtain the right job, he will be successful.'

not teachers of English. Particularly, Chapter 7, entitled 'Command of a Language', outlines a suggested classroom procedure for all subjects. It is based on the proposition that 'what is rehearsed thoroughly in discussion first does seem to be more manageable should a written account of it become necessary'. There is extended comment on the relationship between speech and writing. (Again see Chapter 2 of this book.)

Issues raised by the quiz (Panel 6.1) The use of a quiz to probe one's own assumptions on this topic was first introduced by staff of the Open University in their Language and Learning Course, 1977. This quiz is a development of that idea. Five of the questions are ones they used, and further commentary on them may be found in the relevant study units (Open University Course E262, Block 1). After completion of the quiz, discussion is often animated. Arguments may be informed if not resolved by seeking out the following references, itemised by the number of the statement in the quiz:

Statement 1: See Chapter 5 of Quirk's book. The point is also considered by Wilkinson, and by Trudgill.
Statement 2: See Unit F8, 'How we use Slang' from *Language in Use*.
Statements 3, 4, and 5 introduce the whole question of standard English and so lead to the three books by Mittins, by Trudgill and by Quirk.
Statement 6 and others may also introduce the question of 'appropriate' English as distinct from 'correct' English. See p.50 of Wilkinson, 1971, and 'Speaking Correctly', Unit F9 of *Language in Use*.
Statement 7: See Wilkinson, 1975, Chapters 21 and 22.
Statement 8 should lead naturally into Chapter 2 of this book, and Statement 9 into Chapter 3, but see also the passage about 'Command of a language' in *Exploring Language*.
Arguments over Statement 10, about why teachers mark, will require further study of Chapter 1 in this book, and Statement 11 is a direct reference to Ansell Greene's book *Pullet Surprises,* Scott

Panel 6.4 *A case for correction?*

Should a teacher 'correct' pupils' speech? Which, if any, of the following would you correct, and why, or why not?

1   'How did you get on at the match?'
      'We won them two-nil.'
2   'What's all this fighting about?'
      ' 'E pinched me book, Miss.'
3   'Who did it?' 'It were 'im, sir.'
4   'Do you reckon Henry V was a good king?'
      'I reckon he was a lousy king.'
5   'What do you do on a Saturday morning?'
      'We usually go up town.'
6   'What did you say?'
      'I said, 'oo's 'at's that? It ain't mine.'

Which of the following (if any) would you correct if a pupil wrote it?

1   'He might of thought different if he had come next day.'
2   'We had a fabulous time at the party. It were great.'
3   'Caesar's trouble was that him and Brutus couldn't get on.'
4   'Amoebus don't have no special shape.'
5   'The colonies what Britain used to have are now mostly self-governing.'
6   'Hitler didn't ought to have invaded Poland.'
7   'We didn't have no bovver at the match.'

Forsman, 1969. Are howlers signs of stupidity, or of intelligence?

For a condensed discussion of Statement 12 see the two books by Trudgill and by Sinclair Rogers.

Issues raised by the other panels In Letters to the Press (Panel 6.2) one of the letters is from a student of linguistics, and that study has entered into discussion of what may previously have been regarded as just 'common sense'. Conflicting versions of that 'common sense' recur in arguments about pronunciation, and may affect a teacher's response to his or her pupils. Hence the need to examine the legitimacy of those versions, as Mittins and Quirk do in the aforementioned chapters of their books. The tendency in current thinking is against viewing certain pronunciations as correct and others as deviant.

The issue is a particularly sensitive one when it comes to the 'correction' of children's speech (Panel 6.4). If it is ever right to correct a child's speech, it is important to be sure of our ground in doing so. The sound of his speech is important to the individual: he is at home in it; it is intimately related to his sense of who he is, to his self-esteem and sense of dignity. It is not easily altered. Teachers can, nonetheless, make clear the consequences (in social terms) of using non-standard English when circumstances call for the standard forms. Ideally a pupil should be at ease with both and understand the appropriateness of each in its context.

The extract from George Eliot's *Middlemarch* (Panel 6.5) may help to consider the question: Can we *ever* equate slang with bad/incorrect English? Could slang ever be the 'best' English? Are there distinctions to be made between the spoken and the written word in this respect? If so, what implications might such distinctions have for the assessment of written work? See also *Language in Use*, Unit F8, 'How we use slang'.

Panel 6.5 *Thinking about slang. People often object to slang. Why? Write down a number of words or expressions that you feel to be slang, and then decide in what circumstances (in what places, and with which people) you would* not *feel free to use them. What words or expressions would you use instead? Would these alternatives be in some way better than the slang, or simply different?*

An extract from <u>Middlemarch</u>, by George Eliot.

'But' - here Rosamond's face broke into a smile which suddenly revealed two dimples. She herself thought unfavourably of these dimples and smiled little in general society. 'But I shall not marry any Middlemarch young man.'
'So it seems, my love, for you have as good as refused the pick of them, and if there's better to be had, I'm sure there's no girl better deserves it.'
'Excuse me, mamma - I wish you would not say 'the pick of them.'
'Why, what else are they?'
'I mean, mamma, it is rather a vulgar expression.'
'Very likely, my dear; I never was a good speaker. What should I say?'
'The best of them.'
'Why, that seems just as plain and common. If I had had time to think, I should have said, 'the most superior young men'. But with your education you must know.'
'What must Rosy know, mother?', said Mr Fred, who had slid in unobserved through the half-open door while the ladies were bending over their work, and now going up to the fire stood with his back towards it, warming the soles of his slippers.
'Whether it's right to say 'superior young men' ', said Mrs Vincy, ringing the bell.
'Oh, there are so many superior teas and sugars now. Superior is getting to be shopkeeper's slang.'
'Are you beginning to dislike slang, then?', said Rosamond, with mild gravity.
'Only the wrong sort. All choice of words is slang. It marks a class.'
'There is correct English: that is not slang.'
'I beg your pardon: correct English is the slang of prigs who write history and essays. And the strongest slang of all is the slang of poets.'
'You will say anything, Fred, to gain your point.'
'Well, tell me whether it is slang or poetry to call an ox a <u>leg-plaiter</u>.'
'Of course you can call it poetry if you like.'
'Aha, Miss Rosy, you don't know Homer from slang. I shall invent a new game; I shall write bits of slang and poetry on slips, and give them to you to separate.'

7 The Subject Teacher in a Multicultural School

Allan Jones and Norma George

For a long time urban areas of Britain have been the centres of settlement for groups from overseas. Recently these groups have included speakers of Gujerati, Punjabi, Bengali, Urdu, Cantonese, Hakka, Italian and Polish, as well as of Caribbean Creoles. Initially it was thought that these children placed in English schools, mixing with English children and being taught by English-speaking teachers, would easily assimilate English in the way that a young child does. This was soon proved to be an erroneous assumption. So a range of provisions for educating these minorities was made. These included dispersal, withdrawal for extra language work, and adaptation of remedial and mainstream English. However, many second language learners still failed to achieve their potential.

Many specialist teachers are aware that their second language pupils have the intellectual ability but not the language to follow examination courses. Their response is to simplify the language, but simplification alone will not help the child's language development in the long term. What is needed is a structured approach to the language content of the specialist subjects. If this were done across the curriculum, second language learners, and incidentally many mother tongue English children, would receive language tuition for all the time spent in lessons, instead of the few hours a week they spend with their English teacher. This chapter offers a few practical suggestions for such a policy, as well as attempting to show some of the commonest pitfalls into which the second language learner can fall.

First look at the scripts in Panel 7.1, written by fifteen-year-olds who each had a picture to describe. Why did they make the particular mistakes that they did? Some of the difficulties are with tenses of verbs, where the newcomer to the language does not have the wide range of options available to the native English speaker. Notice for example that one of the girls, Hasina P., used only the present continuous ('The girl is playing. She is enjoying' and so on). Hasina S. used the present simple as well, and Indira used the present simple (correctly) and the present perfect (incorrectly): 'they are happy ... they got a smile on their face'. (Her meaning in this case is of course clear — see the previous chapter.) The other girls used all three forms of the present tense — simple, continuous and perfect — but only Amina used all three correctly.

There are other differences from what a native

Panel 7.1 *Describing a photograph (fifteen-year-olds, for whom English is a new language).*

```
I've got a picture of two girls in the front reading by themself and a girl
siting folding her arms.  Right girl is taller than left girl.  there are not
pencils or pens on the desk.                          (by Amina)

There are three boys standing next to each other.  There are trees at the back
and they are standing on the grass.  And one boy is tall than the others.  And
they are happy they got a smile on there face.          (by Indira)

There are two teach's they have put on their sari's one teacher is sitting on
a chair she is drinking orange.  The are some biscuits in a plate and some
dishes on a table and spoon's folk's.  she have put on a ring. (by Hawa)

The girl is playing a skipping rope and she is smileing and she is enjoying
her self in the playground.                          (by Hasina P)

Their is a boy in the picture and he is runing after the ball.  He has got his
p.e. kit on and he is in the playground.              (by Hasina S)
```

Comments written by a fourteen-year-old for whom English was not her mother tongue. How could more support be provided for her in her ordinary lessons?

Biology
Biology was an interesting subjects but the reason I dont think its useful is because the words and the things we did, didn't interest me. I found Biology very hard and didn't understand it.

Buissness Studies.
Buissness Studies would have been an interesting subjects but the reason I didn't like it was the teaching. It was difficult to understand, some hard words. There was no other way I could use this lesson without understanding.
After school.
I am hoping to work in an office.

Panel 7.2 *Using a camera and developing tank (sixteen-year-olds, new to English).*

```
We first used the filmwinder to wind the film in to the empty film box
then we put the film in to the camera and toke some photo and then he
winded the film back and took it out befor he took photo or put the film
in camera he cut the film.

befor he took photo he went in dark place and he asked use to stay where
the light shins on your face the he took the photo

We used a bag to make it dark so the film wouldent get rouend and we used
spiral to put liquids round it to wash it and he used tank to wash the
film and then we used developer to make the film come out nice   Fixer is
camical



The small barol went into the large barol we then cloused the barol and
turnd the hand bol round we hared tics.  each tic is one photograph.  We
pout into it about ten photograt.  Then we took the small barol out of
the large barol and placet it into the cammerro but we first clipt a bet
of the end and then it went into the cammerro.

We tuck the film out of the camera and placet it into the spiral.  The
spiral went into the tank and add Developer to it after that we put in
Fixer.  Then we washt it with water and hagd it to bry.  This took about
15 minets.
```

English speaker would write, for example the omission of prepositions ('The girl is playing a skipping rope'). Sometimes there is a lack of agreement between noun and pronoun, as when Amina writes about 'two girls ... reading by themself'. Sometimes comparative words are incompletely understood ('one boy is tall than the others'), and the definite article is sometimes left out ('right girl is taller than left girl'). These are just some of the difficulties that learners can experience when encountering English for the first time, and of course most secondary school pupils are at levels of language above those shown here. However, a teacher is more likely to help if he or she knows which aspects of the language they have mastered and which not, so perhaps your first job is to scan their writing with this in mind.

Panel 7.2 shows descriptions by two sixteen-year-old boys of how they used a camera and a developing tank. Notice the past tense forms in the first of the two accounts, *toke* for *took, winded* for *wound,* and *shins* for *shone.* In a technical or scien-

tific account of such a process it would be common to use the passive voice ('The film was put into the camera', and so on). Neither of these boys uses such constructions spontaneously, and if he is to gain a mastery of technical English his teacher will have to consider when and how to help him gain confidence with them. There are also errors in the use of personal pronouns, *use, your* for *us, our,* and prepositions, *befor* for *before,* and the definite article is missing in some places, *tank* for *the tank, developer* for *the developer.* In the second account, past tense forms also caused difficulty:

cloused	for	*closed*	*clipt*	for	*clipped*
turnd	for	*turned*	*placet*	for	*placed;*
hared	for	*heared*	*washt*	for	*washed*
pout	for	*put*	*hagd*	for	*hanged*

Notice also the lack of discrimination between 'b' and 'd' sounds:

hand-bol	for	*handle*
bry	for	*dry*

There are some problems with vowel sounds too, for example *bet* for *bit.*

Some of these problems arise because the writer is transferring language habits from another language, and the following notes may help you to discern such influences and to see that 'mistakes' are not just random carelessness.

Languages from the Indian sub-continent You might find one or more of the following tendencies in children who speak an Asian language at home:

(a) Omission of the definite and indefinite article, usually because their own language makes no use of them: *I went to park* (I went to the park).

(b) Inappropriate use of prepositions: *The boys are on the water* (The boys are in the water).
In several Asian languages the corresponding words are not prepositions at all, but post-positions, coming *after* the noun to which they refer.

(c) Using a wrong order of words: *This girl is* (This is a girl). In the home languages, the usual order is subject-object-verb.

(d) Confusion of tenses: *I finish* (I have finished). In this case the speaker seems to have picked out the 'content' word that carries most of the meaning, but has not yet gained command of the various auxiliary verbs used in English. Consider your own experience in learning any foreign language you have attempted.

(e) Confusion of pronouns and sometimes omission of the plural 's' from nouns: *He hit me* (She hit me), *pen* (pens).

(f) Reversals in clustered consonants: *deks* (desk), *crips* (crisps), *deksis* (desks).
These are usually sounds which they meet in another *order* in their language. (Notice how we find *Dvorjak* difficult, though *advice* is easy!)

(g) Approximations for some sounds: *sip* (ship), *sells* (shells), *vind* (wind), *wase* (vase), *geeve* (give).
These are sounds which cannot be heard easily by Gujerati speakers, as they do not exist in that language. For Bengalis the problem is reversed: *shall* (sell), *showing* (sewing).
There may also be difficulty with English diphthongs if the home language uses pure vowels, and with sounds such as *dh, bh, gh,* and *kh,* which do not exist in English but are common in the Indian language.

(h) An inappropriate selection of register: for ex-

ample *You must give me a job* (Can you give me a job?).
The cultural awareness of when to say what, and in what way, takes time to acquire, especially where different auxiliaries are involved, as in this case with the choice between must, can or may.

Chinese and Vietnamese children Many children from Hong Kong and Vietnam who are now in Britain speak Cantonese. Where that, or Vietnamese, is the home language, you may notice the following difficulties:

(a) The use of 'telegram English': *China book* (the Chinese books).
This probably arises because the home language does not have inflexions for making a word plural, or to indicate a gender change, or (as in this case) to make an adjective from a noun.

(b) Omission of tense changes: *I sell* (I sold, I shall sell, I am selling, and so on).
The verb in Cantonese and Vietnamese has only one form. Word order, and other words, are used to indicate time and object. The lack of small 'code' words makes the contrast with English greater than for speakers of the Indian languages.

(c) Listening for pitch and tonal changes.
In English there are many different ways of saying 'Yes' (see Chapter 4). In Chinese and Vietnamese, however, one tone or pitch is associated with one word or syllable, and attaches different meanings accordingly. In mastering English these children have to find that a change in tone or pitch does not denote word change, though it can affect the meaning of the sentence.

(d) Dropping consonants: for instance, *Wha' hi'?* (What's this?)
These languages have very few consonants coming at the end of a word, except for *m, n, ng* and soft *p, t* and *k*. They may also have difficulty with clustered consonants, where they may not hear and distinguish the component sounds because their language does not cluster consonants: for example, various errors for *stra*ight and twe*lfth*.

(e) Omission of articles: *I go shop* (I am going to the shop).

The influence of Caribbean dialects These are forms of English which diverge sharply from standard English. The differences are not just of pronunciation and accent but involve the grammar as well.

(a) Since pronunciation is very different there may be problems with understanding and using standard English: for example, *hat* and *hot* sound the same in Jamaican English, so do *bud* and *bird*.

(b) Change of tense may not be shown in the words themselves: for example, *tri buda go a dakta* (Three brothers went to the doctor).
Here the past tense is not indicated within the sentence.

(c) Plurals may not be shown by inflexions: for example, *di pus* (the cat), *di tu pus* (the two cats).

(d) The organisation of a sentence can be different: *die biebi niem winstan* (The baby's name is Winstan, or The baby is named Winstan). 'Niem' is difficult to categorise precisely as a noun or verb.

In different parts of the Caribbean there are different creoles, some more influenced by French than by English: for instance, *go a dakta* (went to the doctor) — English based, *ale en vil* (went to town) — French based. The amount of creole influence upon the speech of a person living in Britain depends on numerous factors. Contacts with original creole speakers and the peer group are especially important. The ability to speak a particular creole can be an important sign of cultural awareness and identity, and there are now specific creoles showing the influence of local accents in Britain, for example a Birmingham creole. (See the note in the previous chapter about the problems in 'correcting' the speech of adolescents.) Once they have established fluency in both, speakers can usually distinguish easily the appropriateness of using the creole, or standard English, in different situations. Within Britain, consequently, many children of Caribbean origin are really 'bidialectal'. They move from one dialect of English to another with ease, unless they have recently arrived.

How can a subject teacher help?

Of course it is advisable to find out as much as possible about the children you teach. For a teacher faced with a multi-ethnic class some awareness of who they are and what that means in terms of language experience is just as important as knowing about any past experience that they have had in learning a particular subject. It may be crucial in helping you to ensure that language mastery and subject knowledge grow together, each helping the other.

In addition to the usual information, try to find the regions from which their families come, and the languages and dialects they speak at home. You will find the following agencies helpful in providing guides to the backgrounds of ethnic minority groups:

Your *Local Education Authority Advisory Service.* Some authorities have *teachers' centres* to deal with such enquiries. Universities, polytechnics and education colleges often have staff with an interest in this field, and collections of current books on both language and cultural diversity.

Parents are an excellent source of genuine information. Pluck up courage and ask them.

The *Commission for Racial Equality* and the local *Community Relations Councils* have produced a mass of material especially for teachers. Meet your local Community Relations Officers and use their materials. There is sometimes a small charge for booklets. Each publication deals with specific issues, for example, notes on the names of Asian children.

The National Association for Multiracial Education. Join this organisation or use its materials. Most of what NAME produces has come from practising teachers. There are local groups in many areas with working parties which you can join. Their national conference each Easter is well worth a visit.

The Coordinating Committee for Mother Tongue Teaching. This body specialises in information and working parties on multi-lingualism. Don't be afraid to enquire, even if you only speak English!

It is often found that children who achieve well in their mother tongue also develop well in English. The real problem is with those who learn one language to the age of five, and English after that. They do not develop literacy in their mother tongue and yet they remain behind normal language development in English. There is a good case for overcoming this problem through a bilingual education policy. Teachers interested in following this line of enquiry should read Carl Dodson's *The Bilingual Method* and contact the Coordinating Committee for Mother Tongue Teaching. Addresses of the above organisations are given at the end of this chapter.

Panel 7.3 *Drawing on other cultural backgrounds in the teaching of specialist subjects. A few examples for a school in an area with many Asian Muslims.*

Subject	Topic	Materials To Use In Class
Biology Chemistry	Starch	Samples of rice, chapatti-flour. Diet sheets for different countries.
Maths Art	Tessellating shapes	Pictures of Islamic tile patterns.
Maths History	Time measurement	Information on other calendar systems and astronomical observations.
Physics	Resonance	A sitar or other instrument, and someone to play it.
Physics Biology	Sound	A recording of the muezzin's call to prayer.
R.E. Maths Geography	Comparative religion. Timetabling. Where Mecca is/ Points of compass.	Prayer mat. List of times for local mosque.
Geography History R.E.	Travel Transport	Study of Hadj (Pilgrimage).
Geography Social Studies Science	Comparative dress. Functions of clothing.	Garments (shalwar, kamis, dupatta).

Other aspects of cultural influence

Many speakers of Punjabi, Urdu, Gujerati and Bengali living in a predominantly English-speaking community have now accepted into their language large numbers of English words, such as television (telly), gas, electric, etc. This means that the form of the Asian language spoken at home is changing. Because of this, and since many Asian children born in Britain do not read or write in their mother tongue, parents and community leaders frequently feel the need to bolster the status and development of the mother tongue. This is reflected in the extra schooling many Asian children get. For Muslims it is at a Mosque school, and Sikh and Hindu groups also arrange special classes after normal school hours. Teachers should be aware of this extra teaching and the fact that it may affect a child's ability to cope with homework or to concentrate in school. If there is a complete division between their experience out of school and their learning of your subject in class, then the one is unlikely to help the other.

One way of ensuring that there are more effective links is to make reference within your own lessons to aspects of the relevant culture and to encourage the study of them as a means to understanding the concepts in your subject. For some communities, such as Muslims or Sikhs, your starting point could be the calendar of festivals celebrated in that community, or the foods, clothing and customs associated with them. This could lead you into the history of these cultures, and information on how they have influenced the subject you are teaching (marked, for example, in mathematics). Panel 7.3 gives some examples for a school serving an area with a Muslim community.

> *Take a topic in your own subject. Consider a particular local community you know. Make a list of possible aspects of its life which could be studied with a view to illuminating important concepts.*

There is a danger of labelling children from a particular community, and applying to them folk-wisdom about their culture rather than getting to know more about the particular children you teach. For example, it is frequently said that the single-parent matriarchal family and common law marriage are the norm in Caribbean communities, but this should not be taken for granted. Many pupils will be ready to discuss the religious life of their groups in great detail. Similarly, the overt hostility shown by some Caribbean children to schools and anything which is 'part of the system' should not be written off as just 'bad' behaviour. Their attitude to life might be considered a welcome break from the over-serious view that some educationists have of themselves. Chinese children are also often seen as a single group. This is a mistake. Although Cantonese was described above, there are other important languages (such as Hakka). The life of the individual family is very important to the Chinese child, and the teacher should find out about that particular family. Try asking a Chinese child to teach you the game of Chinese chess, or make a class project out of the Chinese New Year. As with other groups, they have much to offer in a multicultural class.

Writing

When you are dealing with a new topic, try to consider the problems created by new language as well as new content. Many of the pupils will not have mastered the techniques of writing extended passages. Therefore written work should contain plenty of tasks at a simpler level. You could sequence them, gradually introducing more difficult ones.

Here are a few ideas, roughly in order of difficulty:
(a) Provide a set of pictures for them to put in order.
(b) Provide pictures in order, with a set of sentences to sequence underneath (one or two for each picture).
(c) Use pictures in order, with a set of related sentences, this time to be put into a paragraph.
(d) Give pictures in order, and some words which are to be used to construct a set number of sentences explaining the pictures e.g. four pictures, six sentences.
(e) Use pictures in order with questions. The questions can contain vocabulary which the children will use in the reciprocal sentences.
(f) Give out some questions, with sentence answers, in mixed order.

Panel 7.4 *Parts of a matching task. Match the pictures to the right part of the instruction.*

1   Remove the film from the camera
2   Take the film out of the cassette in the dark room
3. Put the film on to the spiral from the developing tank
4   Place the spiral in the tank, and screw on the top.
5   Fill tank with developing chemical.
6   Time how long the developing chemical is in the tank (10 min).
    Invert every minute.
7   Empty developer from the tank.
8   Wash the film with water.
9   Fill the tank with fixing chemical.
10 Time how long the fixer is in the tank. (4 min)
11 Wash the film. (30 min)
12 Take film out of tank and dry it.

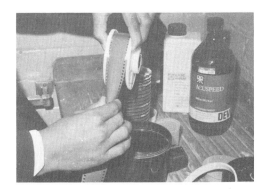

Panel 7.5

---

1. Leicester,

2. 5th April 1978

3. Dear Sir,

4. I am writing to ask if you have any vacancies in your firm for typist tranee

5. I am sixteen year's of age

6. At present I am a pupil at secondary school

7. I am going to take examination for English, maths, R.E. Buisness studies, mothercare and Needlework.

8. I am interest in the work your firm does which is typist trainee

9. I shall be living school on 26th July 1978.

10. I should be grateful if you would give me an interview and I could attend at any time to suit your convenience.

11. yours faithfully,

(g) Provide sentences which are mixed up. Ask the pupils to put them in order to make, for example, a sensible dialogue or a set of instructions.

This technique lends itself readily to use with events in history, cycles in geography, and experiments in laboratories. Some examples are shown in Panels 7.4 to 7.7. *Examine these panels, then by discussion devise a similar task on a topic in your own subject.*

There are lots of ways to help pupils in their writing. Large pieces can be 'built up' from smaller pieces. In the example in Panel 7.5 numbers are used to show the pupil which bits of writing go where in a letter of application. Later the numbers can be left out and the structure of the letter will be remembered. Some useful phrases have clearly been learned. Can you devised a similar task in your own subject?

Panel 7.6 *Parts of a matching task. Topic: acids*

> It doesn't taste sour

> It tastes sour

Panel 7.7 *A sequencing task. How an electric bell works. Put the sentences in order.*

The gong makes a noise.

The hammer is metal. The electro-magnet attracts the hammer. The hammer moves and hits the gong.

Someone presses the switch.

When the hammer moves away from the gong, the circuit is complete again. Electric current can flow again.

The electric current stops flowing. The electro-magnet is not a magnet. It does not attract the hammer now.

Electric current flows along the wires round the electro-magnet. The electro-magnet is now a magnet.

When the hammer moves towards the gong it breaks the electric circuit.

This will happen again and again. The bell will ring until someone stops pressing the switch.

Electric current flows from the battery along the wires.

The hammer moves away from the gong.

Reading material

Consider also the problem faced by learners whose mother tongue is not English when they meet tests and examinations. Some questions set in school examinations and on worksheets tend to confuse even indigenous children. So what chance has the second language learner? Some also presume experience and a cultural background unknown to children from minority groups, and this can also apply to textbooks. Consider the following passage from a book which was being used in a class consisting predominantly of Asian girls.

Vitamin D, *in conjunction with calcium and phosphorus, is necessary for the formation of sound bones and teeth. It helps in the laying down of calcium phosphate in the cartilage of babies and young children during the process of bone formation.*

It is called the calcifying vitamin.

Formation of sound bones and teeth depends on sufficient calcium, phosphorus and vitamin D in the diet.

Effects of a deficiency of vitamin D

Deficiency of vitamin D or of calcium and phosphorus could cause the deficiency disease rickets to occur. Rickets is characterised by the softening of bones due to the inadequate deposition of calcium causing malformation of the bones; symptoms are bow legs, knock knees, etc. Rickets can develop in a baby's body before birth if the mother's diet is deficient in vitamin D. Vitamin D helps to prevent dental decay.

Main sources

Is obtained from two main sources: food enriched by ergocalciferol — a synthetic form of vitamin D — and the action of sunlight on dehydrocholesterol under the skin.

Food.   Animal fats — fish liver oils, especially tunny fish oils, halibut and cod.

Oily fish — herrings, mackerel, sardines, salmon.

Eggs (varying amounts due to hens' diet).

Dairy fats (small supply, more in summer because of effect of sunlight on cows).

Vitaminised margarine (vitamin D added).

Sunlight. Beneath the skin is a layer of fat containing dehydrocholesterol. When the body is exposed to sunlight, dehydrocholesterol is converted to vitamin D — cholecalciferol — which is stored and utilised by the body. Ultra-violet rays cause this change.

Rickets is uncommon in tropical countries, except where purdah operates, but was very prevalent in overcrowded industrial cities in Britain before the cause was known and the cure discovered.

Effect of cooking. *Vitamin D is not destroyed by heat or lost by solubility.*

Its content is certainly relevant for children (and mothers) who may not have been used to the results of Vitamin D deficiency. But look at some of the problems:

(a) the use of passive constructions such as 'is obtained', or 'is characterised by',

(b) long sentences with many subordinate clauses, for example the one that begins 'Rickets is characterised by ...'.

(c) sentences beginning with a preposition, for example 'Beneath the skin ...'

(d) 'difficult' words (as opposed to 'technical' words), for example 'inadequate deposition'.

Try rewriting parts of this text in simple language, and then review the texts available in your own school, perhaps with the help of the measures suggested in Chapter 9.

Acknowledgements

We should like to acknowledge the help of many teachers who have influenced the choice of material and examples given in this chapter, but particularly Alan Pinder, Sue Bond, Benna Odedra and Gloria Straw.

Addresses

National Association for Multiracial Education, 86 Station Road, Mickleover, Derby DE3 5FP.

Coordinating Committee for Mother Tongue Teaching, c/o Runnymede Trust, 62 Chandos Place, London WCZ N4HG.

Commission for Racial Equality, Elliot House, 10-12 Allington Street, London SW1E 5EH.

Further reading

Handbooks prepared by N.A.M.E. and available from the above address, for example:

English and Punjabi: A comparison, by David Gail and K.S. Bath, *West Indian Language: Attitudes and the School,* by Viv Edwards, *Chinese Children in Derby,* by Norman Fitchett.

Schools Council Project in English (SCOPE) *Handbooks I and II,* Longmans, 1969.

Dodson, C., *The Bilingual Method,* Pamphlet No. 9, Aberystwyth University School of Education, 1962.

Ludlow, D.E., *Aspects of Chinese Culture,* Crown Street Language Centre, Liverpool, 1979.

El Said, I., *Geometric Concepts in Islamic Art,* World of Islam Festival Publishing Company, 1976.

'Teaching about Islam' from *Education and Community Relations,* May/June 1976.

For information about the home culture and family life of various minority communities in Britain see the 'Strands' Series of booklets, published by A & C Black, London.

For atmosphere and an understanding through fiction see F. Dhundy's *East End Under Your Feet.*

8 Redesigning a Lesson

Clive Sutton

It is sometimes helpful when planning anything to look at the way someone else did it, and to think how their method could be adapted. In teaching, to see someone else's lesson can stir one's own thoughts. Which parts would work for the class I have? How would I have to alter the approach to fit my style of working? Much can also be learned by seeing the same topic taught by different teachers, and by the same teacher on different occasions. This chapter therefore begins with two lesson descriptions. There are indeed many ways to teach the same topic, and these lessons show something of the freedom and initiative that individual teachers rightly claim. Both relate to the topic of digestion, which appears in the syllabus for both teachers. However, to say they are about the same topic is not entirely true. Is the topic 'digestion' on 'the digestive organs', or what? The two have also been chosen to bring out further aspects of the distinction between 'transmission' and 'interpretation' of knowledge which was discussed in the chapters on writing.

Compare and contrast the two lessons 'The gut of a rat' and 'The problem of digestion' (Panels 8.1 and 8.2). The mental demands made on the pupils in the first lesson are indicated in the time diagram for the lesson. What are the corresponding demands in the second lesson? (For example, are they asked to remember things, to explain in their own words, to suggest explanations, to solve problems, to detect flaws in an argument, to make something, or what?)

For each lesson, which parts can be regarded as predominantly concerned with transmission of information, and which parts are predominantly to enable the pupils to think through, restate, re-express, apply, or otherwise make sense of new knowledge?

Are there any other differences which you consider important? What are the strengths and weaknesses of each of these two lessons?

Perhaps you agree with the authors of the Bullock Report that knowledge can't just be 'handed over' (see page 3). On the other hand, you may think they overstate the case. In some lessons or parts of lessons pupils will be relatively passive recipients of information 'handed out'. This is an important part of teaching and needs to be done well, but at the very least it seems that that will be ineffective unless balanced by other kinds of activity.

Barnes suggested a distinction as follows:

Language seen as mainly for TRANSMISSION of established knowledge	← →	Language seen as mainly for INTERPRETATION of new and unfamiliar ideas in terms of what is already known.
(Clear statements by teachers are therefore the key to learning.)		(Statements by pupils are therefore the key to learning.)

Any particular teacher might have one of these ideas about the functions of language more firmly in mind than the other, or a teacher might alternate in emphasis. On the basis of teachers' explanations of the purposes of written work, how they set it, and what they did with the pupils' scripts, he concluded that there were indeed distinct groups, and in one account he deliberately overstated the extremes by describing two imaginary teachers, thus:

The teacher at the Transmission end of the dimension sees language as a kind of speaking tube: he sends knowledge down the tube, and the pupil receives it or fails to do so. When he asks questions of his pupils, or tells them to write, it will be primarily in order to test whether they have in fact received the knowledge he transmitted. The language tube is now operating in reverse as a source of feedback. This teacher does not see writing as being connected with his pupils' thinking or

Panel 8.1 *The gut of a rat: a lesson with thirteen-year-olds.*

'Oh, sir, we've got you again have we? It's made my day', says Marion good naturedly, as she waltzes, rather conspicuously, to hang her coat on the pegs at the side of the laboratory. The teacher finds her irritating, and tells her off sharply. He takes a register, stopping several times to insist that they settle down and be quiet.

DEMANDS MADE ON THE PUPILS

1.45	To be quiet
	To copy down a title
	To watch
3.00	To copy from the board

After a brief revision question to make a link with the last lesson the pupils are asked to copy a title from the board, 'Looking at the gut of a rat'. Then they gather round to watch. The teacher has the rat and dissection tools ready. 'Now this is a deep frozen rat. Someone tell me what sex it is.' They peer over the carcass with giggles and nudges, but the animal's external anatomy is not very clear. 'Well, it's a female', he says. He starts cutting. His delivery is spontaneous and fluent. By the time he has pointed out the stomach, liver and diaphragm they have settled down and their interest is held.

Periodically there are cries of Ugh! and Uugh! One girl is upset, perhaps ready to vomit, certainly to weep. The teacher notices, and asks Marion to take her out and look after her. Marion takes her to the preparation room, where Mrs L, the laboratory steward, is working.

The teacher goes on describing the parts revealed by the dissection, going into some detail - the caecum, the mesentery. He describes their functions. A few questions are asked, mostly 'What's that?', and he answers them directly. Some of the boys break away in giggly asides and are quelled: 'Shut up while I'm talking.'

Having completed the tour of the abdomen, the teacher cuts through the ribs to show the heart, lungs and windpipe. 'Are you going to do the brain?', asks someone.

After about 35 minutes the pupils go back to their places, and copy notes from the board, followed by a diagram. They chat amongst themselves as they do so, and the teacher rebukes them periodically, urging them to 'get on with it'.

Panel 8.2 *The problem of digestion: another lesson with thirteen-year-olds.*

Four boys arrive early and nose around the demonstration bench, where there is a partially dissected rat covered by a damp cloth. They peer under the cloth and point out to each other the things they know - liver, intestines. 'Where's the kidneys?', says one. 'Are we doing this today?', says another to the teacher, who is sorting papers a few feet away. She nods and carries on with what she is doing, but after a while diverts two of the boys to write on the board a full list of what they ate for lunch. The rest arrive. The teacher points out the lists on the board, and asks questions about what foods are for. 'For energy', 'They help you to grow', and so on. She points out that although the boys' arms and legs are certainly growing they aren't actually made of lettuce and carrot, or cheese and onion pie, and poses the problem of how 'food stuff' is changed into 'body stuff', and how it gets to the parts of the body where it is needed.

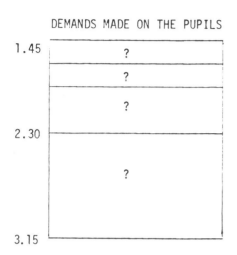

DEMANDS MADE ON THE PUPILS

1.45 ?

?

?

2.30

?

3.15

1.55   After a pause she explains the idea of breaking things down, to make the materials for new constructions. She uses the analogy of house demolition to give bricks and wood and wire, etc., that might be used in a new building, lists these on the board, and then asks the class to make similar lists of the usable parts of cheese and onion pie, OR ham sandwich OR fruit cake. (One group to each food.) As they write their lists she wanders among them, and chides those girls who have listed pastry as pastry rather than fat and starch. A spokesman for one group reads out their list, and the teacher says 'Now we will go on to examine the cheese and onion pie demolishing machinery of a human being ... or at least of a rat...' Some of the boys push John forward, saying 'He'll do, there's no difference.'

2.05.   They crowd around as the rat is unveiled and the teacher quickly traces the digestive system, starting with the teeth. 'What is their part in the whole job?' For some (easy) parts she simply points with a needle and says nothing, whereupon they name them or ask questions ('How long is its intestine?'). She listens, and then offers more description and explanation. She takes a long time to explain what the pancreas does. Finally she points out the blood vessels around the gut and asks for speculation as to why there are so many, and what they are for. Several hands go up, but it's a question just to think about, and the pupils are sent back to their places to start on the following tasks. They can choose which to do first.

(i)   to write down their ideas about the rich blood supply, with reasons,
(ii)   to stick in their books a duplicated diagram, and to write in opposite it what happens in each section of the gut (books available),
(iii)   to identify parts in a photograph of a rabbit's gut, and then draw it,
(iv)   given the length of the rat, and of its intestine, to calculate a likely length of a human intestine.

2.30-3.15.   Pupils writing and talking. Most complete two of them before the bell goes.

understanding. Indeed, he does not think that talking or writing about something alters the way in which one knows it: the knowledge passes up and down the tube unchanged. If he mentions learning in connection with language he will be referring to the accumulating or memorizing of information, or the handing-on of techniques. He will tend to see his responsibility when he receives written work in terms of assessment; this done he will take no more interest in it.

The teacher at the other extreme of the dimension will emphasize language as a means of interpretation. He will see discussion and writing as ways of helping pupils to think more effectively, and will credit them with ability to make sense of experience for themselves by talking and writing about it. For him knowledge is something which each person has to make for himself. As a teacher he tends to be very aware of his pupils' attitudes to the work that he gives them. He is careful to be a good audience to his pupils; he writes comments on his pupils' work, often reads it aloud or displays it, and uses it as a springboard into the next piece of work for the class.[1]

More sympathetically towards the teacher at the transmission end, we might say he is a person who is fascinated by the subject, believes he has a lot of exciting information to convey to his pupils, and whose way of doing this is by talking a lot to them. He spends a lot of time explaining and trying to convey the nature of problems and their solutions. The teaching process tends to be one-way, with the pupils listening most of the time. He wants them to share what he knows, and to understand and remember it.

On the other side is the teacher who is sceptical about what children can learn by listening, and takes a delight in seeing pupils wrestle with an idea for themselves. He provides provocative things for them to talk or write about, formulates problems, stimulates them to discuss, with each other and with him, possible solutions. He spends a lot of time listening and questioning, and little time telling.

Barnes takes trouble to point out that these are extreme stereotypes, and that a teacher may operate between them, or for good reasons shift from one to the other at various times, but he does bring out clearly the different theories of knowledge implied, and you might consider what your own ideas on this are:

One teacher
(a) Believes knowledge to exist in the form of public disciplines.
(b) Perceives the teacher's task to be the evaluation and correction of the learner's performance.

Another teacher
(a) Believes knowledge to exist in the knower's ability to organise thought and action.
(b) Perceives the teacher's task to be the setting up of a dialogue in which the learner can reshape his knowledge.

As a result of these differences knowledge at present taught in our schools seems to be an amalgam of two kinds — bodies of knowledge handed over, and knowledge which the learners are required to reshape and make suitable for influencing their own lives. What is the value of each? Barnes does not propose that teachers should never present knowledge in lectures, but leaves to you the professional decision of how much of that to do and how much interpretive activity to try to arrange.

Meaning expansion

To talk of theories of knowledge in the context of teaching must raise the question of what we imagine might be happening when someone acquires new thoughts. What do *you* think goes on inside a pupil's head when he or she comes to learn or understand something?

One possibility is simply that something is *added* to a store. But if so, where in the store will it go? Our subjective experience is of connections to other things we know, and indeed new knowledge is easier to cope with when we have, as it were, somewhere to file it. With that in mind the early stages in coming to know a new topic should probably involve a clear survey of the general outlines. This can give the pupil an overview of the main ideas, a means of organising his thought when talking, reading and writing about the details later. For a discussion of this approach to 'meaningful learning' see the writings of David Ausubel.[2] He is concerned with the growth of a *structure* of understanding, and suggests that the most important thing in a child's ability to learn is what he already knows and how it is organised. The teacher has an important job to do in discerning parts of his pupil's existing pattern of understanding so that he can identify points at which the new ideas can be attached. In the case of a totally new topic there may be very few suitable points of attachment in the child's thought, and therefore the clarity of the teacher's first organisation of the topic, and his or her ability to find some 'cognitive bridges' to the child's earlier experience, are crucial.

One way of trying to get an insight into a child's present pattern of connected ideas is by means of 'burr' diagrams. A key word from the topic of the day is written in the centre of the page or blackboard, and gradually surrounded by other words which spring to mind as the pupils talk about it. The method has been more used by English teachers than by those, for example, in science or history, but it has something to commend it in all subjects. Incidentally it offers a useful corrective for anyone who thinks that the meaning of a word is a fixed thing, the same for everyone. The details of what a word or idea 'means' to one person are often very different from what it means to another. For a child, or anyone else, meaning also changes over time. Unfamiliar words are meaningless at first, if they make no connections to old knowledge. If they trigger a few associations to things one already knows about they can take on a little meaning, and thereafter that meaning can be gradually enriched by making more and more connections. Some possibilities for two common words are shown below.

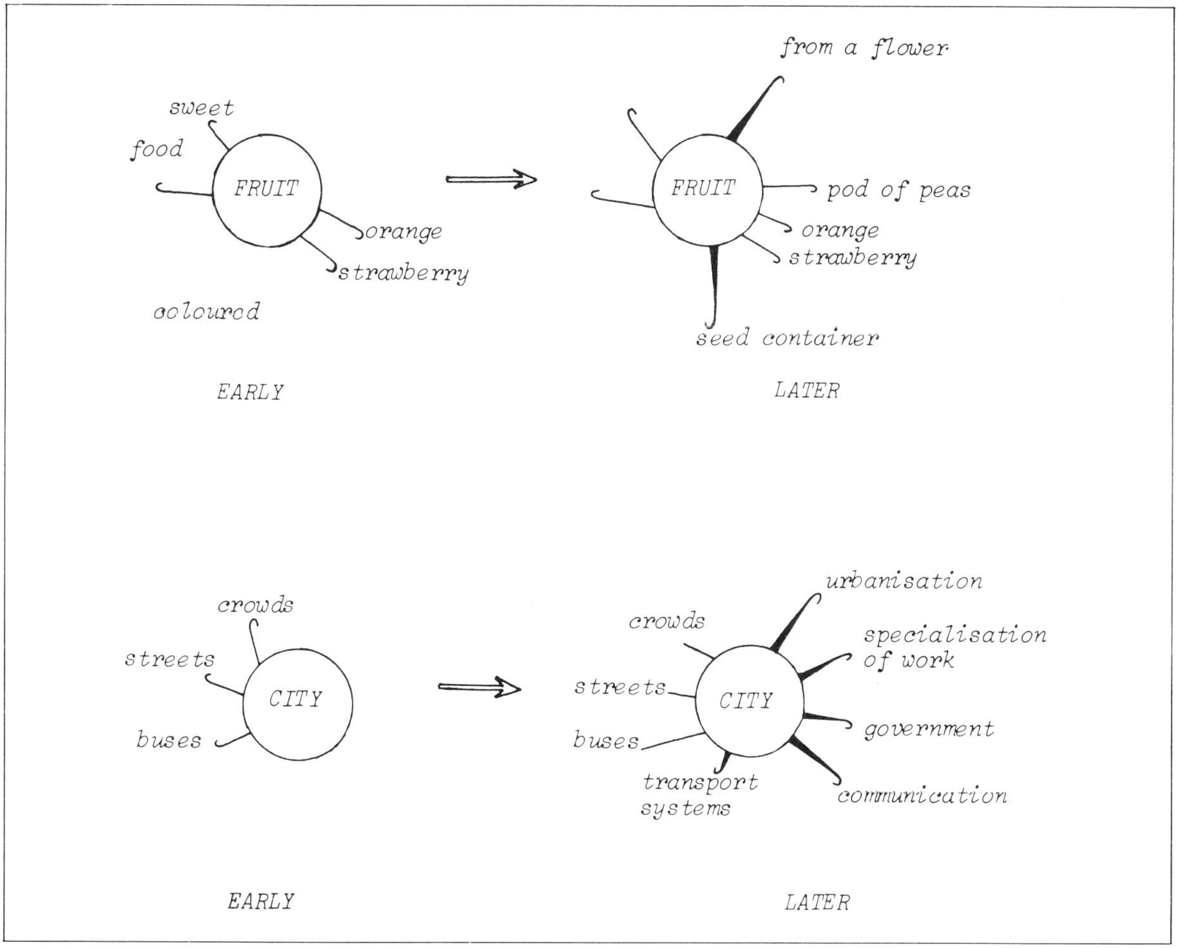

The biology teacher hoping to teach the idea that fruits are seed containers developed from flowers could help his own awareness as well as that of the children by having them draw a 'burr' at the beginning of a lesson. The word 'burr' is itself a reference to those dry fruits with hundreds of hooks on them, and the diagrams show a progressive acquisition of new connections, even if only a few of the many hundreds which a person may have.

You can check these ideas from personal experience by observing your own efforts, or those of your pupils, to make sense of 'nonsense' words. What kind of creature do you suppose an amphisaurus to be? Where would you expect it to live? What does costulitis mean to you, and how do you go about trying to clothe it with meaning? Do you make new connections on hearing that anti-costulitic drugs are expensive?...and so on.

The multitude of associations and connotations, some trivial, some vividly important, form a part of the meaning of words which has frequently been regarded by subject teachers as somehow less important than the denotative meaning: the definition. This is probably because they have a specific job to do in strengthening the key connections which contribute to the denotative meaning. (Some of these are shown in bolder lines on the diagrams.) A biology teacher will rightly concentrate on the idea of a fruit as a seed-container developed from the ovary of the flower, so that the pupil comes to see what tomatoes and pods of peas have in common with apples, pears and peaches. A geography teacher may rightly concentrate on those features of a city which delineate the rational, logical, concept of a city. But in both these cases there are a wealth of connotations, a rich 'penumbra of meaning' for these words from pupils' background experience out of school. For the learner it is the myriad of these associations that make the meaning, and one might see the teacher's job as managing their growth. Certainly it seems to be a misunderstanding to regard them as peripheral and dispensable, since it is often these connotations which give reality to the idea because they make it tangible or visual. They also enable recollections from outside school to be 'brought to mind' and related to the matter under discussion. The school knowledge may then indeed have some bearing on what they really know and understand. To take another example, the meaning of 'voltage' is not captured in its entirety by a statement or definition in a book. For one child it may include memories of the alarm on the teacher's face when someone wanted to connect his apparatus to the mains, for another it includes memories of elaborate warning notices seen on pylons, of a meter she has used, of torch cells, and so on. To plan a physics lesson on

Redesigning a lesson

Read the lesson description in Panel 8.3 and then write a plan for an alternative lesson on the same topic, which would allow either better exposition by the teacher or more scope for interpretive activity. Better still, take a lesson outline from teaching materials in your own subject and treat it similarly. You might like to work with another person and plan two contrasting lessons that make best use of the strengths of each approach. Try to state the demands you hope to make on the pupils' reasoning.

Some school-based enquires

1 Find occasions where children are using language to talk through a new idea, or to think it through in writing, and to reassess their existing understanding in the light of new knowledge.

Prepare a short account of an example, illustrated where possible by photocopies of their scripts or verbatim extracts from what they said.

2 'Children are more involved in their own work when they are given the opportunity to talk about their own relevant experience.'
'Children are seldom given an opportunity to formulate a viewpoint different from their own.'

Choose one of these statements made by commentators on contemporary secondary schools. Bear it in mind for a period of at least a week in school. Whenever you can, note down evidence which tends to support or to contradict it. In what circumstances is it true? Prepare a short report on your findings.

Panel 8.3 *A lesson on advertising, with young school leavers aged fifteen and a half.*

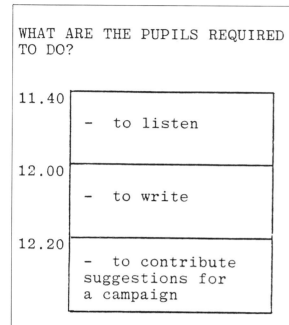

WHAT ARE THE PUPILS REQUIRED TO DO?

11.40	- to listen
12.00	- to write
12.20	- to contribute suggestions for a campaign

The teacher stands beside the board and presents his analysis of advertising techniques, writing on the board as follows:

1 ASSOCIATION OF IDEAS
a) We don't buy beer, we buy friendship.
b) We don't buy cigarettes, we buy manliness, romance, prestige.

2 APPEALING TO THE EMOTIONS
a) motherhood   b) sex
c) humour   d) nostalgia
e) escapism   f) acceptance
g) free offers

At each point in his analysis he gives an example of an advertisement which he thinks fits the particular category. Sometimes members of the class chip in with comments such as "That's like the Ansell's Bitter advert", and the teacher nods appreciatively. However, these comments come only from three boys. One of them becomes more confident and volunteers more and more examples of his own, and the others fall quiet.

The teacher then asks them to make a note of the various techniques, and to include some of the examples in what they write. They settle down to do this. One asks what 'prestige' means.

About 25 minutes from the end of the lesson the teacher announces a new task: the pupils are to imagine themselves planning an advertising campaign for a new soft drink - to think of a suitable name for it, plan posters, TV advertisements, etc. He asks for their suggestions, and chairs the "discussion". This time most of them contribute ideas. The teacher comments on these as they come up, and allows the name "Fresshssh" for the drink, as well as the slogan "Get Freshshsh...", but time is running out before any further details are decided.

the basis of knowledge-interpretation and meaning-expansion implies planning for opportunities for the growth and enrichment of these connections.

While these are theoretical points, they bear on the immediate task of how to divide time in a lesson, and what activities to make available.

References

1 This is Barnes' account in *Language in the Classroom,* Open University Study Unit, Course E262, Block 4.
2 Ausubel, D., *The Psychology of Meaningful Verbal Learning,* 1963, and Ausubel, D., *Educational Psychology: A Cognitive View,* 2nd ed. Holt, Rinehart and Winston, 1978.

Further Reading

Carré, C.G., *Language, Teaching and Learning in Science,* Ward Lock, 1981.

9 Appraising a Textbook

Chris Dawson

What makes you reject one book on a library shelf in favour of another? What makes you browse through a particular book in a bookshop? In teaching, what features of a book will determine your decision to use it or not? Many of the features which potentially influence your choice — for yourself or others — are summed up in the general term 'readability'. It encompasses a wide variety of features including the style, size and distribution of *print* on the page, *the presentation of the subject-matter, the complexity and formality of the language,* as well as *the motivation of the reader.*

On the following pages there are extracts from widely used school textbooks (Panels 9.1 to 9.6). Examining these, or some other texts of your own choice, what features of them, if any, would appeal to the pupils?

The complexity of the text

Clearly, readability is not merely a question of how easy the sentences are, and to select only texts with the simplest sentence structure might be quite inappropriate. On the other hand, one would not like pupils' experience of textbooks to resemble the mystification which sometimes accompanies official form filling.[1]

Try checking your general impressions of the chosen books with the help of the following questions:

SUBJECT MATTER — Is it made interesting to the reader?
PRINTING — Do you like the size and style? Does its organisation on the page help the reader?
LANGUAGE — Does it seem to you relatively complex? ... simple? ... formal? ... informal?

What other criteria would you use?

However, many studies have concentrated on the complexity of the text, and have found it a useful general guide in considering how well suited a book is for pupils of a given age range. Perhaps the main impact of these studies is to make teachers more aware of the high levels of demand made by many secondary school textbooks.

Among the features which may contribute to such a high level of demand, the following are just a few of those which have been studied:
The number of words per sentence.
The number of syllables per sentence.
The proportion of words in dependent clauses.

	Minimum reading age
Application form for a Family Income Supplement	13
Application to buy Premium Savings Bonds	16
Application to re-licence a motor vehicle	17
Child Benefit application form	14
Application for civil legal aid	17
Divorce petition	17

Panel 9.1 *From a textbook for twelve-year-olds*

Push-push.   Pull-pull

Forces

A hammer knocks a nail into a wall—a solid has exerted a force. A river washes away a bridge—a liquid has exerted a force. A hurricane sweeps a roof from a house—a gas has exerted a force. Every minute of every day you (a mixture of all three states of matter) are pushing, pulling, twisting, squeezing. *Can you write a list of some of the forces you have exerted in the last few minutes? (1)*

How would you recognise a force if you met one? (2)

Panel 9.2 *From a textbook for thirteen-year-olds.*

Mass, Measurement and Motion

What is a definition? Dr Johnson once defined a network as 'anything reticulated or decussated with interstices between the intersections!' Some dictionary definitions are not very much more enlightening. For example, one dictionary defines a cow as the 'female of the bull', and a bull as the 'male of the cow'. When you were very young a cow was probably any large hairy creature with a leg at each corner. Later you learned to distinguish calves, cows, bulls, and bullocks, and if you are seriously interested you can probably recognise Ayrshires, Friesians, Herefords, Jerseys and Belted Galloways.

In physics, too, we often begin with vague ideas and gradually change to more precise definitions as we learn more about the subject. In your first year, for example, *mass* was the amount of stuff in a body and *force* a push or a pull. In this section we will develop these ideas so that we can measure mass and force.

Panel 9.3 *From a textbook for thirteen to sixteen-year-olds.*

Osmosis

Osmosis can be regarded as a special case of diffusion; the diffusion of water from a weaker to a stronger solution. A weak solution of salt, for example, will contain relatively less salt and more water than a strong solution of salt. Thus the diffusion gradient for salt is from the strong to the weak solution, but for water the diffusion gradient is from the weak to the strong solution. If two such solutions were in contact, the water molecules would move one way and the salt molecules the other until both were uniformly distributed. If, however, the two solutions are separated by a membrane which allows water but not salt to pass through, only water can diffuse.

Panel 9.4 *From a textbook for eleven-year-olds.*

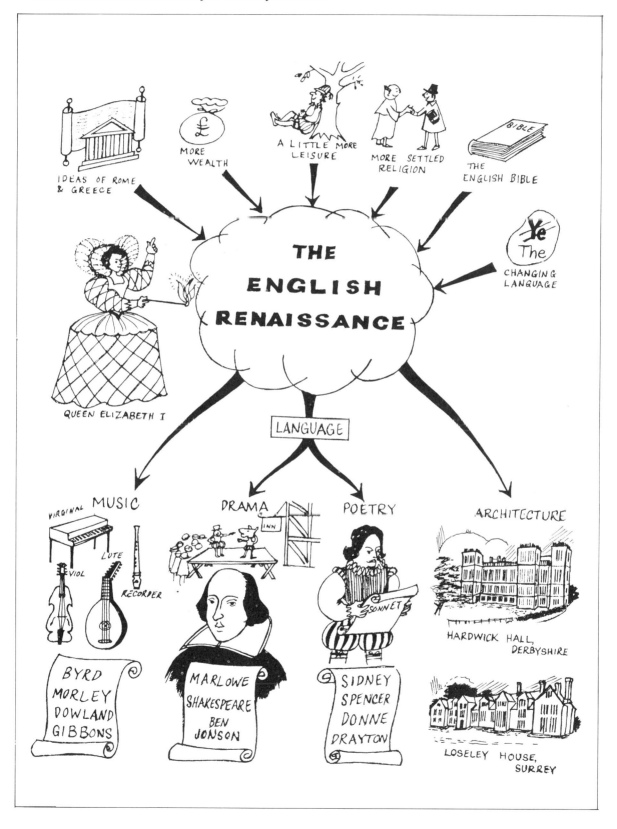

Panel 9.5 *From a textbook for eleven-year-olds.*

FIXING A POSITION

A playground conversation (John and Malcolm are talking).

J. 'There you are, that's the boy who won the cross-country last year.'

M. 'Where?'

J. 'Over there, he's the one with the dark hair.'

M. 'I can see lots of boys with dark hair.'

J. 'Well you see the gate, don't you?'

M. 'Yes.'

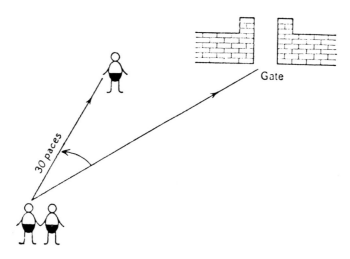

J. 'Well now turn a little to your left, and you will see that he is about 30 paces away from us.'

M. 'The boy looking down now?'

J. 'Yes, that's him.'

This method of fixing a position depends on naming a landmark first (the gate), then talking of a turn and a distance. It works quite well over a short distance but is not very accurate. Why not?

The proportion of sentences complete in one line. The proportion of 'uncommon' words (words absent from various published lists of the most frequently used English words).

The frequency of abstract nouns.

The ratio of technical to non-technical words.

The frequency of personal pronouns.

The proportion of linking words and phrases such as 'moreover', by contrast,' and so on.

Studies of this kind have resulted in a number of 'readability' formulae. We need not concern ourselves here with the working-out which produced them, save to say that behind them lies a vast network of statistical correlations between writing styles and comprehension tests. Our concern here is with how they work, and whether or not they can help the teacher. Most of them take into account either vocabulary or sentence length. One finding of the Schools Council Project on 'The Effective Use of Reading' was that these, and word length, are the best overall indicators of difficulty. Details of some of them follow on pages 114-17.

Panel 9.6 *From a textbook for A level students.*

No town, however, is independent of the effects of changes in the cultural situation upon which the value of its physical setting depends. Cultural change must inevitably either strengthen or weaken the original value of the site and situation of each and every town. By creating new human needs and new capacities it is responsible for the emergence of fresh places as favourable localities for urban development, and for the obsolescence of others that were formerly auspicious. The weakening tendency, however, may be retarded or even largely overcome by human capacities of adaptation. Since the establishment and growth of the town have fixed capital, both material and social, at a particular place, diminution in the value of the physical setting is only exceptionally followed by evacuation. Human groups show extraordinary resources in overcoming growing handicaps to their continued occupation of an established site. Confronted with the alternative of moving or of striving to overcome mounting difficulties and disabilities a community almost invariably chooses the latter, and usually with a considerable measure of success. Yet when a survey of urban fortunes is extended over a long period of time, or its equivalent a period of accelerated or revolutionary cultural change, the distributional adjustments in the urban pattern are clearly apparent. The mill of geographical circumstance grinds surely, if sometimes slowly. Urban centres which have really profited from successive radical changes in human organization and technology, as distinct from those which have survived them, are few in number and deservedly great. These favoured few have proceeded from strength to strength, accumulating population, wealth and prestige.

The Flesch readability measures

Rudolph Flesch, an American authority on readability, approached the problem from two angles, trying to identify the *reading ease* and the *human interest* of a text. A word of caution: a readability score doesn't exempt the teacher from making decisions about the appropriateness of the written material so far as unquantifiable features are concerned, such as subject-matter, conceptual level, legibility, the child's own interest, or indeed, whether or not the material is comprehensible. It is quite possible for a piece of writing to be readable, but not to make sense. Make sure your attempts to simplify difficult material or to write 'readable' worksheets don't lead you into 'nonsense'.

(a) Select three textbooks you know. Put them in a notional order of difficulty. Then measure their reading ease by means of the Flesch procedure, explained below, and the Fry method. Do your results agree? How much variation is there when you use different passages from the same book? Note these measures are intended only as a guide to the level of demand made by a book.

(b) Rewrite, at an appropriate level, a passage which you have estimated as being too difficult for your class.

(c) Try to get some pupils to rewrite a difficult passage (see later in this chapter). How does it differ from the original?

To calculate the Flesch index of Reading Ease.

Choose about five passages at random from different parts of the book. In each one, mark off a hundred words and complete the following counts. Hyphenated words, contractions and abbreviations count as single words. For sentences, follow units of thought rather than punctuation. Sometimes colons or semi-colons mark the end of a sentence.

		Random passages chosen 1st 2nd 3rd 4th 5th	Average
Total number of syllables in 100 words	Bk A Bk B Bk C		- - - - - - - - - - - -
Average number of words per sentence	Bk A Bk B Bk C		- - - - - - - - - - - -

GLUYAS
WILLIAMS

Panel 9.7

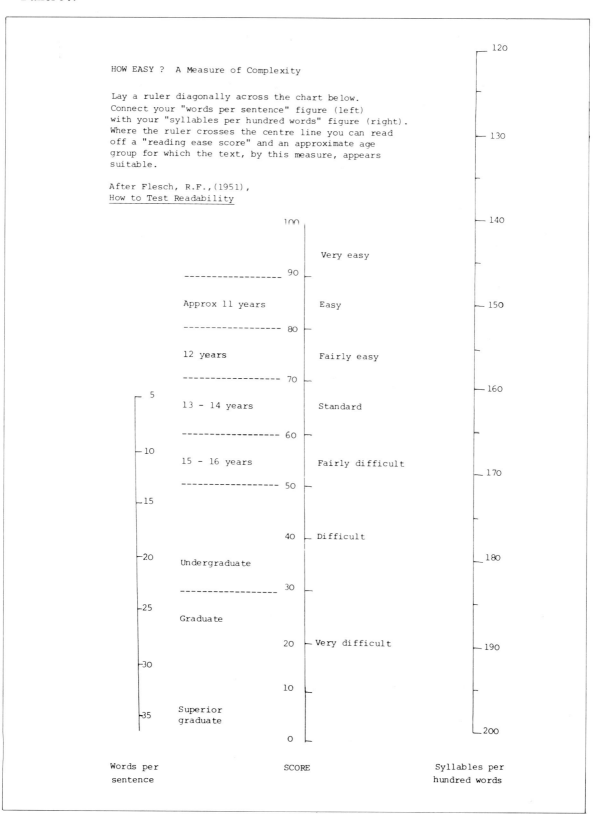

HOW EASY ? A Measure of Complexity

Lay a ruler diagonally across the chart below.
Connect your "words per sentence" figure (left)
with your "syllables per hundred words" figure (right).
Where the ruler crosses the centre line you can read
off a "reading ease score" and an approximate age
group for which the text, by this measure, appears
suitable.

After Flesch, R.F.,(1951),
How to Test Readability

Words per sentence		SCORE		Syllables per hundred words
		100	Very easy	120
	Approx 11 years	90	Easy	130
	12 years	80	Fairly easy	140
5	13 - 14 years	70	Standard	150
10	15 - 16 years	60	Fairly difficult	160
15		50	Difficult	170
20	Undergraduate	40		180
25	Graduate	30	Very difficult	190
30		20		200
35	Superior graduate	10		
		0		

Panel 9.8

HOW INTERESTING ? A Measure of Human Interest

The other component of the Flesch Readability Formula is the attempt to measure <u>human interest</u>. You may find fault with this part of the formula, but it does represent an attempt to measure a feature which is deemed to be significant even though it is acutely difficult to measure.

The human interest score is based on a count of personal words and sentences. A detailed definition of what constitutes a personal word and a personal sentence can be found in the original source.*
As a general indication, take personal words to include personal pronouns (I, we, you) and words that have masculine or feminine gender (John, Mary, father, sister). A personal sentence is conversational. It includes remarks to the reader and exclamations.

Lay a ruler across the following chart to connect your personal words figure (left) with your personal sentence figure (right). Where the ruler crosses the middle scale read off the Human Interest Score.

* Flesch, R.F. (1951), <u>How to Test Readability</u>

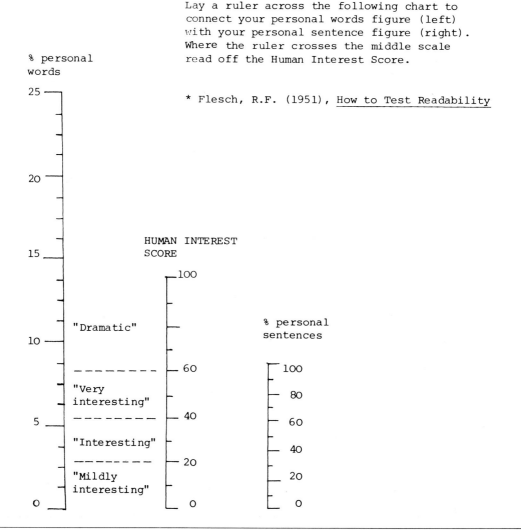

Panel 9.9

A GRAPHICAL METHOD FOR ESTIMATING READABILITY

(After Edward Fry, Rutgers University Reading Centre)

Randomly select three one-hundred word passages from the book you are testing. Plot on the graph below the average number of syllables and the average number of sentences. The graph will then show Fry's estimate of an age group that will cope well with this text. (For details see E.A. Fry (1968), "A Readability Formula that Saves Time", Journal of Reading II, 7, p513.) His original specifications were in grade levels for American schools, i.e., what appears below as 6-year-olds was his Grade 1, etc. By his measures a plot coming near to the trend line is likely to give a more reliable indication than one far from it. Choose more passages per book if great variability is observed.

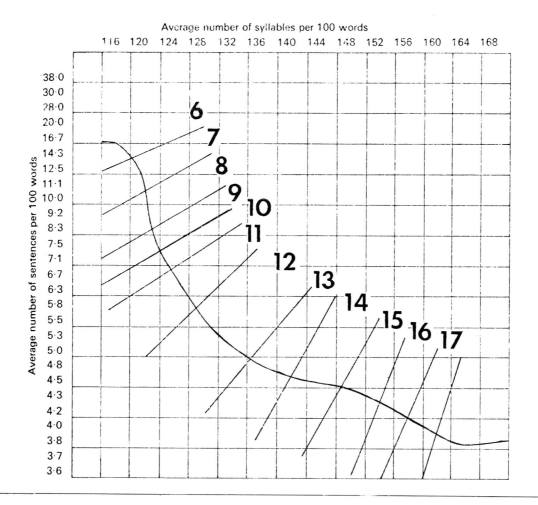

Matching the text with the learner

The above procedures do not actually check the text with the particular pupils you have in mind. An alternative method which does allow for this is the *cloze* procedure.[2] A passage from the book is typed out, but with a number of deletions. The difficulty of the original passage is estimated by finding what percentage of the gaps the reader can fill with the original word or a satisfactory alternative.

You can experience cloze procedure for yourself using the passage in Panel 9.10. Note that the first and the last sentences in the extract remain intact, and that every seventh word is deleted. This is a typical, though not the only, cloze procedure. There can be two types of deletion: structural and lexical. With the former, every 'nth' word is deleted. A lexical deletion, by contrast, entails the elimination of a word from a particular grammatical class, such as all the nouns or verbs in the selected passage. The following chart provides a guideline for interpreting cloze scores:

65% correct	*Independent level. Ability to work with and understand the text.*
40-65% correct	*Instructional level. Likely to require some teacher support.*
40% correct	*Frustrational level. Difficulty in using text even in a very supportive classroom.*

The cloze procedure has many different uses. It can both predict a reader's ability to work with a text, and assess his comprehension of what he has read. Used as a focus for group discussion it can perhaps help him to comprehend the text more fully. In practice, cloze tests correlate well with other measures of readability, and may indeed be superior to them insofar as they overcome one of the great weaknesses of the other formulae, which are not sensitive to the difficulty of the *ideas* in a passage. A cloze procedure will necessitate the interaction of the reader with the passage in a more complete way. And, of course, there is the added bonus, that cloze tests are fun!

Select a passage at least 175 words long from a book you use with one of your classes, and from which pupils are expected to obtain information without guidance. Use the cloze procedure to determine the number of pupils at the independent level. What implications are there for the teaching of this class?

Panel 9.10 *Experience of cloze procedure. Identify the missing words in the following passage taken from a geography textbook. The answers are given at the end of the chapter.*

Though India has many very large, **growing** cities, by far the greatest number of people still live in villages. India has been settled for many _____ of years, and has been invaded _____ times in history by people who _____ through the mountain passes in the _____ and north-west. Each new invading tribe_____ nation brought into India its own _____ and religion, but they did not _____ destroy the people who lived there_____ them. Often the newcomers would settle_____ in the villages that were already_____ , but since they came as conquerors _____ did not mix with the other_____ , and when there was hard physical _____ to be done the invaders would _____ the other villagers to do it. Then, _____ some later time, the land would_____ invaded again and new settlers would _____ to the villages, so another group _____ form. As the centuries passed, there _____ up what became known as the _____ system. A caste in India is _____ social group or class. Even far _____ in Indian history there were castes. _____ were sometimes of different races - dark _____ light skinned, tall or short, and _____ on. These racial differences are still_____ detectable in Indian society. It was_____ usually allowed for couples of different_____ to marry, and if a person_____ born into a certain class he _____ find he was also born into_____ certain kind of work. If his_____ were farmers, he would be a_____ , if they were shopkeepers he must _____ a shopkeeper, and so on. Sometimes_____ would break the rules, but not_____ . The Hindu religion, which is the _____ important religion in India, allowed castes, _____ often there were different Hindu festivals_____ ceremonies for the different castes, For many Indians today the caste system is part of their religion, although some Hindu priests do not consider it to be so.

Pupils re-writing the text

In 1975, four fourteen-year-old pupils in a South Australian secondary school volunteered to rewrite the chapter 'Organ system of the body' from their science textbook *Science for Secondary Schools, Book 2*. No assistance or guidance was given with this, and they worked in their own time.

Differences between the original text and the version rewritten by pupils

1 READABILITY

(a) The reading level of the original text estimated by using a readability formula was 11th grade; for the rewritten chapter it was 9th grade.

(b) The degree of difficulty the pupils found with the original and the rewritten chapter was estimated by combining a comprehension score with a reading rate.

		Original text	Version rewritten by pupils
Number of pupils	Coping at independent level	0	2
	Coping at instructional level	5	17
	At frustrational level	29	15

2 AMOUNT OF LEARNING

'The test at the end of the unit stunned me. I have never given a test before in which all but seven of the students obtained over 80% ... Students seemed to understand the unit very well.'

(Class teacher's comment)

3 FEATURES OF LANGUAGE USED BY PUPILS

(a) *Using the Expressive* There was a persistent expressive/colloquial flavour to the rewrite. Thus:
'many' became 'a lot of',
'immerse the bone' became 'put the bone in',
'sever the leg' became 'cut the leg'.

(b) *The 'Lay' word versus the Scientific* Pupils showed consistent tenacity in making the learned commonplace. Thus:
'locomotion' became 'moving',
'vertebral column' became 'backbone',
'embedded' became 'buried'.

(c) *Becoming Familiar with the Audience* For instance, the formal 'You have learnt' became a more permissive 'You all know'. The impersonal 'the bones of the arms and legs are attached' was personalised to 'your arm and leg bones are joined'. The unqualified 'obtain a large meat bone' is made more realistic: 'obtain a bone (if you can) from your butcher'.

(d) *Reducing the 'Frinstances' and Analogies* It was interesting to note the ruthless way in which the students worked like marauders to cut out a good deal of the corroborative and illustrative detail while retaining the key ideas. This is consistent with the general tone of down to earth and cut the sideshow! Pupils dismissed the supposedly helpful analogy between circulation of blood and of traffic, and wrote: 'The circulatory system is the only way that the blood can pass through and around the body.'

(e) *Getting straight to the point* Allied to the reduction of explanation was the use of direct, active language, where the text tends to be indirect and in the 'passive voice'. Contrast the textbook's: 'The contraction of a muscle results in the movement of a bone' with the pupils': 'when the muscle contracts, the bone moves'.

(f) *Pre-empting* While textbook writers and teachers may think it desirable to stimulate pupils to speculate or to challenge them to think, it seems that these pupils believed in making the known facts immediately available. Thus where the text asked: 'Where are the ribs located in the skeleton of a snake?', the pupils, not with the greatest precision, said: 'A snake's skeleton goes from head to tail!' And the possible hopeful textbook question: 'Can you explain your observation?' was replaced with: 'Write down what happens'.

(g) *Blurring the Precise* The textbook read: 'Large muscles ... are firmly attached to bones by bands of inelastic tissue called *tendons*.' The rewrite read: 'The larger muscles are firmly attached to the bones by bands of unstretchable tissue called tendons.'

(h) *Getting excited* One textbook instruction read: 'Before the blood dries, examine the slide under your microscope.' The pupils wrote: 'Then quickly put it under the microscope.' That word quickly is perhaps a bit of a maverick in a science text; it hints at the excitement of the experiment and the little drama of the laboratory.

(i) *Aping the Scientific* While the pupils are mainly intent on secularising the language of science, there were instances where they did the opposite. Thus the text explained that 'the trachea finally divides', while the pupils somewhat amusingly stated: 'the windpipe finally bissects [*sic*] into two smaller tubes'. An interesting, if not entirely appropriate, transfer of a geometrical concept.

References

1 Data on the reading ages for official forms: *Legal Action Group Bulletin,* February 1977, p.31.
2 Taylor, W. L., 'Cloze Procedure: A new tool for measuring readability', *Journalism Quarterly,* 1953, pp.415-33.

Bibliography

Bormuth, J. R., 'Validities of grammatical and semantic classifications of cloze test scores', in F. J. Allen (ed) *Reading and Enquiry: Proceedings 10,* International Reading Association, 1965.
Flesch, R. F., *How to Test Readability,* Harper and Row, New York, 1951.
Fry, E., 'A Readability Formula that saves time', *Journal of Reading,* 1968, p.513.
Gilliland, J., *Readability,* Hodder and Stoughton, 1972.
Gunning, R., *The Technique of Clear Writing,* McGraw-Hill, 1952.
Harrison, C., 'Assessing the Readability of School Texts' in Lunzer, E. and Gardner, K., *The Effective Use Of Reading,* Heinemann, 1979.
Harrison, C., *Readability in the Classroom,* Cambridge University Press, 1980.

The omitted words in the cloze passage were:
thousands, many, came, north-east, or, customs, entirely, before, down, there, they, people, work, make, at, be, come, would, grew, caste, a, back, They, and, so, sometimes, not, castes, was, would, a, parents, farmer, be, people, often, most, and, and.